Basic
LEATHERCRAFTING

All the Skills and Tools You Need to Get Started

Elizabeth Letcavage,
editor

Bill Hollis,
leathercrafter
and expert consultant

Photographs by
Alan Wycheck

STACKPOLE
BOOKS

0 11557 03617 6

Published by
STACKPOLE BOOKS
5067 Ritter Road
Mechanicsburg, PA 17055
www.stackpolebooks.com

Printed in China

10 9 8 7 6 5 4 3 2 1

First edition

Cover design by Tracy Patterson
Top left cover photo: designs by Tandy Leather Factory.
Clutch purse, page 184: made by Bill Schiefer, designer un-
known. All other designs by Bill Hollis.

Library of Congress Cataloging-in-Publication Data

Basic leathercrafting : all the skills and tools you need to get
started / Elizabeth Letcavage, editor ; Bill Hollis, leathercrafter
and expert consultant ; photographs by Alan Wycheck. — 1st ed.
    p. cm.
  Includes bibliographical references and index.
  ISBN 978-0-8117-3617-6 (alk. paper)
  1. Leatherwork. I. Letcavage, Elizabeth.
TT290.H58 2011
745.53'1—dc22
                              2010026231

Contents

Acknowledgements

Thanks to our leather expert's wife, Mary Hollis, who contributed her time and talents to help organize and facilitate project production and the photo sessions.

Appreciation is also extended to Tandy Leather Factory—and the hospitable staff at its Harrisburg, Pennsylvania, store—for providing some of the tools and supplies included here.

Introduction

Leathercrafting is a rewarding activity that combines working with your hands, engaging your mind, and using your creativity. This book will show you how to take a smooth, flat, unadorned piece of cowhide and transform it into a decorated three-dimensional piece of practical art.

Begin by familiarizing yourself with the tools of the trade. The first chapter provides a starting point for assembling what you need to complete your first project. You'll find that many tools are specific to leathercrafting and available in varying degrees of quality and price. When it comes to tools, buy the best you can afford. The best tools will truly produce the best results.

The techniques chapter will guide you through every procedure that goes into constructing leather goods—from selecting leather to applying a final finish. You'll learn the fundamentals of tooling: selecting and preparing the leather, transferring a design, carving the leather with a swivel knife, embellishing the design by making impressions in the leather with stamps, coloring the leather, and using finishing techniques to impart a professional look.

These techniques are put to use in the final chapter, which covers making a belt and card case. The same skills and techniques used to make these items may be used to complete a variety of other projects, such as guitar straps, dog collars and leashes, gun belts, tool belts, and equestrian tack. Make the card case, and then you can move on to wallets, checkbook covers, media player and CD cases, notebook covers, and much more.

As you work with leather, you'll quickly discover that practice leads to perfection and experimentation results in excellence. If you carve and stamp regularly, your leatherworking technique will improve, and so will the final product. Develop your own style, try new ways of working your projects, and invent tooling designs that are different from what you see in the marketplace.

Your handmade leather goods will be greatly appreciated gifts. And, because they will last for decades if well cared for, they often become treasured family heirlooms. Each piece of smooth, flat, unadorned leather is a blank canvas ready for you to create a one-of-a-kind masterpiece. Enjoy the experience!

1
Getting Started

An article in a 1945 issue of *Popular Mechanics* encouraged readers to try leathercrafting. "Few tools are needed," said the writer, "and most of these can be made from nails, bolts, nutpicks, and other common objects." Years later, when the craft became more popular, the Tandy Leather Factory began selling the "Lucky Seven," a collection of essential carving and stamping tools that is still available.

There's no need to fashion your own tools today— machine-manufactured tools are affordable and widely available. While many leathercrafting tools are specific to the craft, there are suitable substitutions for some, and these are noted throughout this book. Where possible, we've offered alternative methods of completing a step so that the purchase of a tool that might only be used occasionally isn't necessary.

Some suppliers offer several types of leathercraft starter sets. These "workshops in a box" include basic tools and supplies along with project kits to make such items as a wallet, checkbook cover, key chain, and the like. Generally speaking, they are a good value, especially if they are on sale. Tool quality can be on the low end, however, and you will want to pass over sets aimed at children.

If you decide to take up leathercrafting as a lifelong hobby, you will likely want to add to your collection and trade up for the more expensive tools. If you're lucky enough to have a leathercraft specialty store nearby, take advantage of specials and clearance-priced merchandise. Consider, too, joining a leathercraft club sponsored by leathercraft specialty stores and online vendors. They offer members generous discounts and regular specials.

If you don't live near a store, everything you need is available online. Refer to the Resources section for a list of suppliers that offer everything you need.

1

Leather is best stored loosely rolled with the grain side facing inward, and always in a dry place.

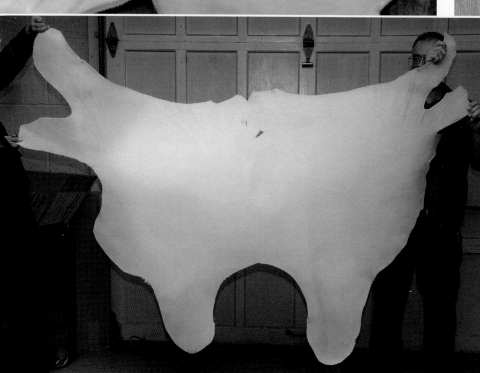

Many leather projects can be cut from this double shoulder hide.

The belly—located on the sides of a double shoulder hide—is the least expensive part of a hide and prone to stretching. For that reason, it is not recommended for good quality leather work. It is the best portion to use, though, for projects that are to be molded into three-dimensional items. It is also suitable for kids' projects and sometimes used to make small stamped items.

Leather for Tooling

Tooling is the art of carving and stamping designs on leather goods. The only type of leather suitable for tooling is *full grain* and *vegetable tanned.* Full grain refers to a cow hide that has had the hair removed ("top grain" leather, which is unsuitable for tooling, has been sanded to remove imperfections). Vegetable-tanned leather has gone through a tanning process that uses vegetable matter, tree bark, and other natural materials so it doesn't decay.

Tooling is done on the smooth *grain side* of the leather. The underside is referred to as the *flesh side.* The price of a hide goes up based on the quality of the grain side: *economy* hides may have holes, barbed-wire marks, brands, and stains; *good quality* hides may have slight blemishes and imperfections; and *excellent quality* hides are almost blemish free.

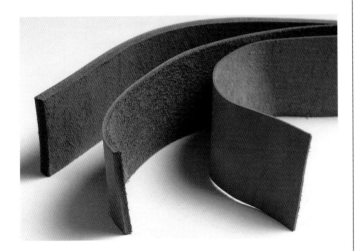

From left to right: 8-ounce, 6-ounce, and 4-ounce leather strips are $^8/_{64}$-inch, $^6/_{64}$-inch, and $^4/_{64}$-inch thick, respectively.

Leather thickness is expressed in ounces. To create a uniform thickness, the hides are split with a machine. Leather that measures $^1/_{64}$ inch (0.0156 inch) thick equals 1 ounce. So a weight of 5 ounces means that the hide is $^5/_{64}$ (0.0781) inch thick. A 6-ounce hide is $^6/_{64}$ (0.0937) inch thick.

A split cowhide is rarely the same thickness throughout. Because there will be slight variations throughout the hide, it will be sold in a weight (thickness) range. A 5- to 6-ounce hide means that some parts of the hide may be $^5/_{64}$ inch thick while others may be $^6/_{64}$ inch thick. The heavier (thicker) the hide is, the higher the price.

Vegetable-tanned leather is sold by the section and priced by the square foot. Modern tanneries use a computer program to measure the usable portions of a hide, so you won't be paying for any holes. The hide measurement in square feet is usually indicated on the flesh side of the hide.

Basic Hide Sections with Corresponding Sizes in Square Feet

Belly: 4 to 8 square feet

Shoulder: 5 to 7 square feet

Double shoulder: 11 to 14 square feet

Back: 15 to 18 square feet

Side: 21 to 28 square feet

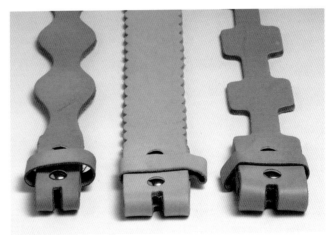

Beginning leathercrafters are well served by the variety of precut belt strips and blanks available. Some blanks have prepunched holes and others are complete with snaps and a belt keeper. The unique geometric-shaped blanks above would be very difficult to cut by hand. Strips and blanks are also available in sizes to make dog collars and hatbands.

Project Kits

KIT ADVANTAGES

- Leather pieces are precut and punched.
- Kits include a tooling design pattern and instructions for project assembly.
- Special hardware (zippers, metal belt clips, snaps, and so on) is included.

KIT DISADVANTAGES

- Leather quality can vary within a kit and from kit to kit and may have slight blemishes.
- Project must be laced or stitched as determined by the prepunched holes, and those holes may be irregularly spaced.

Tandy Leather produces a large assortment of project kits available through its own stores, other leather-craft suppliers, and large craft stores. Kits eliminate the preparation work so you can start tooling right away. They enable a beginner to produce a fairly advanced item with less work.

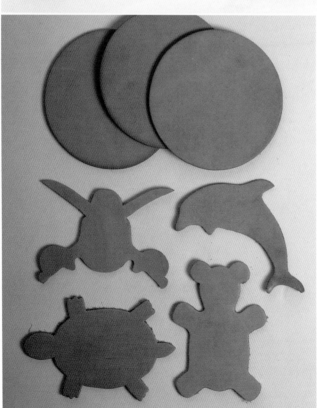

Many precut leather shapes are available. The "rounders" are great for carving and stamping practice and for testing dyes.

Leather retailers sell bags of remnants, sometimes called "off fall," that may be used for small projects. Off fall pieces are also ideal for practicing stamping and carving and testing dyes and finishes. Of course, if you cut large projects from a hide you will have a collection of free off fall for smaller projects.

Specialty Leathers

LINING LEATHER

To line a small project, 2-ounce or 3-ounce full-grain, vegetable-tanned leather may be tooled or used as is. Other options include chrome-tanned cow hide, pigskin, kidskin (goat hide), and sueded versions of these hides. Lining leather is sold the same way as cowhide: by weight and square feet. Prices and selection vary between specialty stores and online vendors, so search around to get what you like at a fair price.

HAIR-ON HIDES

These are very expensive and generally used as floor coverings or to upholster furniture. If you come upon a deal at an auction or find a damaged hide, however, you can use small pieces as an insert in a tooled CD case, notebook, binder, and the like.

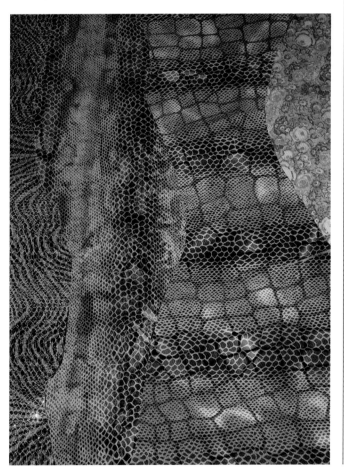

SNAKE SKINS

Authentic or man-made snake skins are used to cover belts and for accessories and inlay work. Authentic skins are pricey; synthetic ones, less so.

GARMENT LEATHER

Garment leather is often chrome tanned, predyed, soft, and flexible. Although it cannot be tooled, it can be used to line projects such as handbags and cosmetic bags. Don't overlook fabric stores as a source for real and synthetic garment leather.

The Work Surface

Tip: Our expert uses contact cement to adhere a Poundo Board to a stone slab, creating a double-sided surface.

A good leathercrafting work surface starts with a sturdy table large enough to give you space to maneuver and have easy access to your tools. Although a card table will suffice, a better choice would be a table that won't wobble while you are stamping. Keep in mind, too, that the surface could be marred by an accidental dye spill or knife gouge, so the table should not be an heirloom or antique.

Good lighting is essential. Supplement natural light or overhead lighting with a swing-arm lamp. Such lamps are inexpensive and can be found at craft, hardware, office supply, or large discount stores. Some have a heavy base while others have a clamp that attaches to most table edges. Energy-saving fluorescent bulbs provide more light and less heat, making them more comfortable to work under.

As you work, you'll want to keep your work surface clean. Leather is very delicate when wet and easily marred. Be sure there are no metal chips, filings, or residue on your work surface. Ferrous metals, which include steel and iron, react to the chrome salts in leather and can cause permanent marks.

Once you have your table and lighting in place, you'll need three additional portable surfaces for stamping, cutting, and punching. These are available specifically for leather working, but there are suitable substitutes.

RUBBER MAT

A hard rubber mat protects your work surface and punching tools. Placed under your tooling slab, it absorbs noise and vibration from repeated mallet strikes. Mats sold commercially are called Poundo or Protecto Boards. Some leathercrafters use a heavy (8 to 10 ounce) piece of tooling leather underneath their work. Another option is a linoleum flooring square. True linoleum, as opposed to thin, sticky-backed floor tiles, can be found at stores that specialize in flooring materials.

POLYETHYLENE CUTTING BOARD

Protect your cutting blades and work surface with a textured polyethylene cutting board. These are sold in discount stores, kitchen shops, and grocery stores. A smooth-surface plastic or acrylic board allows work to slide, so choose a textured board.

STONE SLAB

A hard, heavy, smooth granite or marble slab is ideal for using when carving or stamping designs on leather. Slabs for leather tooling are usually made of granite and available in 12-by-12-inch or 12-by-24-inch sizes. Both are $1\frac{1}{2}$ inches thick.

Suitable substitutes include 2-inch-thick natural flagstone or slate from a garden store. Another possibility is man-made solid-surface acrylic countertop material (sold under many brand names), found at building supply stores.

Leathercrafting Tools

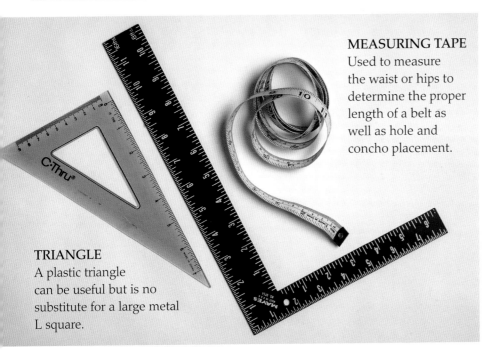

MEASURING TAPE
Used to measure the waist or hips to determine the proper length of a belt as well as hole and concho placement.

TRIANGLE
A plastic triangle can be useful but is no substitute for a large metal L square.

L SQUARE
A measuring tool with a 90-degree angle is essential for cutting a square piece of leather and making precise angles. Hardware stores offer the most options for this must-have tool. An 8-by-12-inch version is a practical size for many projects. Squares with a longer arm are useful when marking and cutting large cowhides into belt strips. If you have an uncoated steel version, protect it from moisture, as a rusted tool is impractical for leather work.

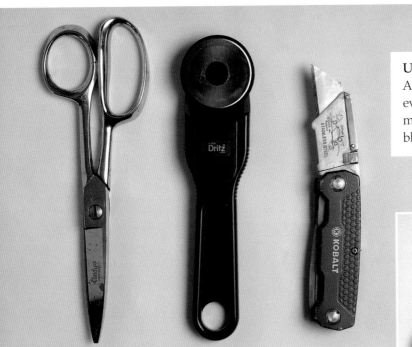

UTILITY KNIFE
A handy tool for cutting leather strips, evening up an edge, trimming lace, and much more. Keep plenty of replacement blades in stock.

LEATHER SHEARS
Ordinary household scissors are not suitable for leather. Find heavy-duty shears specifically made for leatherwork at leathercraft suppliers.

ROTARY CUTTER
An ideal tool for cutting lining leather, a rotary cutter can be run along a metal ruler to cut a straight line or used freehand to cut curves. Keep a supply of replacement blades on hand. A heavy-duty model is best.

WING DIVIDERS
Indispensable for determining correct spacing, transferring measurements from a ruler, and scribing lines on leather. A moderately priced set (under $20) will work for the leathercrafter. You can find them at woodworking and drafting supply stores. A well-worn tool will also work as long as the locking nut isn't loose.

SKIVER

"Skive" means to thin down or pare. In leatherwork, skiving is used to remove the surface of the leather where a fold will be made or reduce the thickness of two pieces of leather that will be joined. A skiver can be purchased at leathercraft supply stores and through many online vendors. (There is a French edge skiving tool that will make a small channel, but the tool shown here is more versatile.)

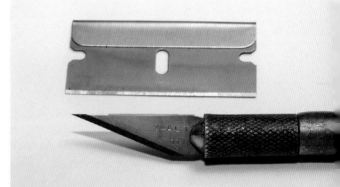

STRAIGHT RAZOR BLADES

Razor blades are used for small jobs, such as trimming the ends of lace, and larger tasks, such as cutting a glued lining from a tooled project piece. They must be sharp for best results, so have plenty on hand.

CRAFT KNIFE

A craft knife has many light-duty uses. The popular brand X-ACTO features an aluminum handle and easy-to-replace blade. A good choice is a #1 X-ACTO handle and a #11 blade.

ROUND OR HEAD KNIFE

Professional leatherworkers and avid amateurs cannot get by without this tool. It's more expensive than the other cutting tools but does a better job and can replace the rotary cutter, strap cutter, utility knife, and skiver. Get a good one.

SCRATCH AWL

Most woodworkers have several of these in the toolbox. In leatherwork, it has multiple uses: scribing lines, centering patterns, punching small location holes, and more. A moderately priced version is adequate for leathercrafting.

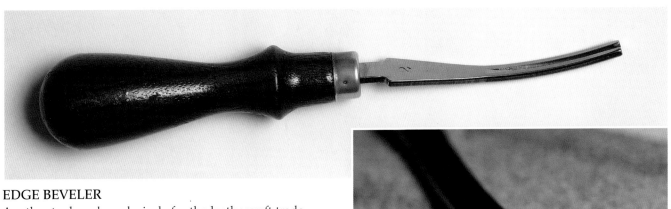

EDGE BEVELER

Another tool made exclusively for the leathercraft trade. Used to round off edges to achieve a neat finished appearance, bevelers come in various sizes to accommodate different leather thicknesses. A size 2 edge beveler is a good starter size. A good-quality beveler is worth the investment; cheaper versions tend to tear the leather rather than cut it.

TRANSPARENT RULER

A see-through ruler is handy when you are selecting an area of a hide for a project.

SINGLE-HOLE PUNCH AND HOLE PUNCH SETS

Round and oval hole punches are needed for belt making. Single punches or multipunch sets are available with interchangeable tubes. They range in size from $1/16$ to $3/8$ inch. Their uses include making billet holes and holes for attaching snaps and rivets. Oval holes resist stretching better than round ones, so the recommended punch for belt billet holes is a $1/4$-inch oval punch.

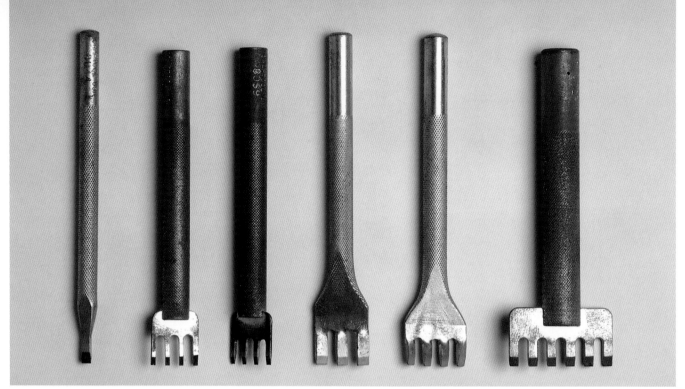

LACING CHISELS

These tools stamp slits for flat lacing. They are available in prong widths of $3/32$ and $1/8$ inch with straight or angled prongs. (To lace the card case in this book, you will need a $1/8$-inch width one-prong chisel and a $1/8$-inch width three- or four-prong straight line chisel.

BELT STRAP END PUNCH

These punches make precision belt end cuts. They can be used on belt straps of varying sizes. If you like to make belts, you will want to add these to your tool bag.

OBLONG PUNCH

An oblong punch, also called a bag hole punch, makes a perfect hole to accommodate the tongue of a belt buckle. They are available in five sizes, from $1/2$ to $1^1/2$ inches.

ROTARY PUNCH

Allows you to select from a range of hole sizes. While a budget-priced model will work on light leather, a deluxe model is required for heavy-duty work. This tool is used only for narrow items such as belts and straps (The belt project featured here calls for a $1/4$-inch single hole punch; you can use a $1/4$-inch tube from a punch set or the $1/4$-inch punch setting on a round-hole rotary punch.)

SWIVEL KNIFE

A leathercraft supply specialty item. The standard model is chrome plated with a steel blade. Deluxe models are made of stainless steel. The steel blade (right, top) will need to be sharpened periodically with a sharpening stone, while the slightly more expensive ceramic blade (right, bottom) will never need to be sharpened or honed.(Ceramic replacement blades can be purchased to fit a steel handle.)

WHITE JEWELER'S ROUGE

Jeweler's rouge is a compound made of abrasive material and a grease binder, and is used to polish precious metals. Leathercraft suppliers sell "white" jeweler's rouge: a 2-inch piece will last a long time.

LEATHER STROP

The verb *strop* means to sharpen: stropping will help maintain a sharp and clean edge on your tools. It's done to remove dirt and debris from tools and is not a substitute for using a honing stone to sharpen dull blades. Strops are made of a board to which a leather strip is glued, flesh side up. White jeweler's rouge is applied to the leather. All knives, carving blades, and some leather stamping tools should be stropped before use and repeatedly while in use. This tool is necessary to achieve good-quality leather items.

JEWELER'S FILE

Also called a needle file, this is used to smooth the inside edge of hole punches to maintain maximum sharpness. They are available singly in a specific size or in sets of varying sizes.

RAWHIDE MALLET

Most leathercrafters prefer the feel of a rawhide mallet over a polymer one. Easy to control and "break in" to your style of tapping, they come in various weights (2 to 24 ounces) and head diameters (1 to 2³/₄ inches). A 9- or 11-ounce mallet is a good starter weight.

Rawhide mallets are "dead blow" tools—all of the energy is transferred to the tool head rather than causing the tool to bounce. The heavier the mallet, the less force you need. Lighter mallets may be less tiring to use if you plan to tool for several hours at a time.

POLYMER MALLET

Polymer mallets are less expensive and won't wear out. The disadvantage is that they are not dead blow tools and so they bounce back after striking, which results in less control. Some poly mallets are advertised as having less bounce than others. (A mallet's bounce has no effect on making leatherwork go faster; work speed comes only with experience.)

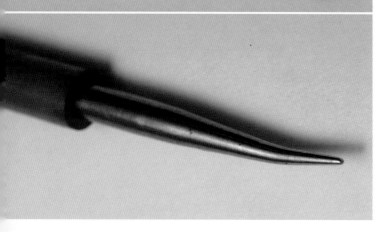

CLEAN WATER AND CELLULOSE SPONGE

If your tap water is drinkable, it's suitable for wetting leather in preparation for stamping and carving. You will also want to have a supply of new household cellulose sponges on hand to apply water or colorants. Plan to use a new sponge with each technique that requires one. Cut them in half with regular scissors, and you will have a perfect palm-size applicator.

SPOON/STYLUS MODELING TOOL

This combination spoon/stylus tool has multiple uses. The spoon end is used for transferring Craftaid template patterns, for figure carving, and to smooth out beveling marks. The stylus end can be used to transfer designs when using transfer film or tracing paper and for tooling.

STENCILS

There has been a huge increase in the range of stencil designs available thanks to the scrap-booking craft. Stencil outlines can be transferred directly onto leather to be embellished with carving and stamping.

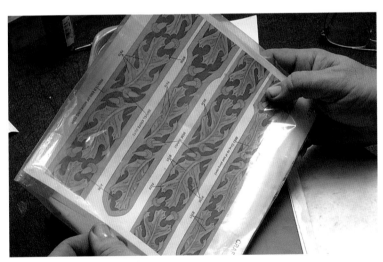

DESIGN TEMPLATES

These Craftaid templates are clear plastic sheets with raised ridges. They produce a crisp, clean transfer. An array of designs is available.

TRANSFER FILM OR TRACING PAPER

Used to transfer a design from a pattern, book, magazine, or drawing to your leather project. Tracing paper is a coated translucent paper that comes in pads. It is more delicate than film but can still be used several times. Transfer film is heavier, translucent, water-proof paper sold by the yard. It is more expensive than tracing paper but is more durable and can be used over and over.

TOOLING STAMPS

Hundreds of reasonably priced stamping tools are now available. In the early days, tools were handmade from nails. In the late 1940s, commercial production began in the United States, with the Craftool Company taking the lead. Most tools sold today are produced in Asia under the Craftool brand name.

New tools have a prefix letter and number stamped on the handle. Purchased design patterns will specify which tool to use to stamp each element of the design. Older Craftool stamps may have just a number (if they were made prior to 1963) or no number at all (made before 1950).

The beginner is advised to use the exact tool specified in the pattern while learning tooling techniques. Once the basics are mastered, older unmarked tools will be easy to incorporate into your work.

Most stamping tools are made of chrome-plated steel. Care must be taken to protect the chrome finish. If it is damaged, the tool is unusable. Don't store tools loosely in a bag or box where they can bang against one another. If you don't have a tool rack, space tools apart on a length of felt or other plain fabric or use a case intended for knitting or crochet needles.

An inexpensive plastic tool rack protects tools and makes them easy to reach. More costly wood racks are also available.

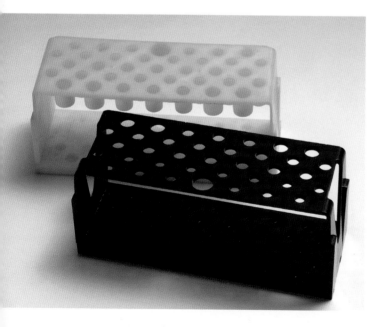

Key to the Code

The prefix letter refers to the category of tool. Even with this system, sometimes the designations differ or are mismarked. Smart buyers will take a good look at a stamp before buying it.

A: Background	**N:** Sunburst
B: Beveler	**O:** Special
BW: Barbed Wire	**P:** Pear Shader
C: Camouflage	**R:** Rope
D: Border	**S:** Seeder
E: Special	**U:** Mulefoot
F: Figure Carving	**V:** Veiner
G: Geometric	**W:** Flower, Acorn, Pinecone
H: Stop	
J: Flower Center	**X:** Basketweave
K: Special	**Y:** Flower Petal
L: Leaf	**Z:** Special Craftool Code
M: Matting	

4-IN-1 AWL SET

Comes with four interchangeable tips: a scratch awl blade, size 2 and 3 stitching awl blades, and a lacing fid blade.

ADJUSTABLE GROOVER

Slices a uniform channel near the edge of the leather piece to accommodate stitching thread. It adjusts to the width of the leather you are using.

OVERSTITCH WHEEL

Does two jobs: It makes evenly spaced thread-hole marks for hand stitching. After the piece is stitched, it is used to set the stitches by rolling the tool across the threads to push them down into the groove. The tool is sold in specific sizes to make five, six, or seven holes per inch. If you are purchasing only one, the six-holes-per-inch size is most useful. (Also available at a higher price is a spacer set that comes with a handle and interchangeable five-, six-, and seven-holes-per-inch wheels.)

THREE-DIMENSIONAL STAMPS

A huge variety of designs is available in the heavy-duty 3-D stamp category. Some specialty sets come with a detachable handle; otherwise the handle is purchased separately. Several styles of alphabet and number sets in various sizes are also sold; these are great for personalizing your project.

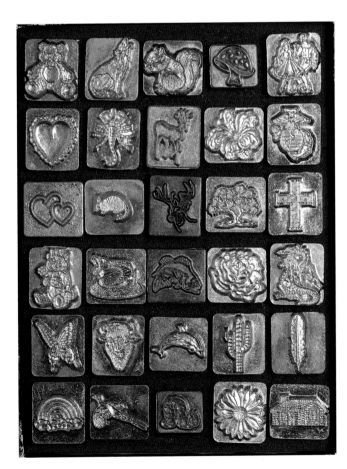

STITCHING THREAD

Waxed linen thread is the best choice. If you don't use prewaxed thread, you must wax it by passing it through beeswax. It's sold in black, natural, and brown. Avoid nylon thread for leather projects; it is not as flexible and tends to cut the leather over time.

STITCHING NEEDLE

Also called saddler's needles, they have large eyes and blunt tips.

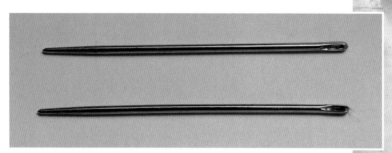

STITCHING PONY

Holds your work firmly during lacing or stitching. Place the horizontal arm under your legs while sitting in a chair. Wing nuts allow you to adjust the pressure to hold various projects.

LACING NEEDLE

These flat needles have tiny spikes to securely hold lace in place. Keep several backups on hand in case you damage the spikes while clamping the lace into the needle. These are available through lace suppliers.

LACE

Don't skimp on lace quality. Buy the best you can afford. Kangaroo lace is recommended; it's available in $1/8$-, $3/16$-, and $1/4$-inch widths, in black, brown, whiskey, and natural colors. Less-expensive options such as cowhide and vinyl are good for practice. These tend to stretch and are more difficult to work with, however.

Adhesives, Colorants, and Finishing Products

APPLICATORS
Wool daubers are a mess-free way to apply stains, dyes, and edge wax. Inexpensive alternatives are lint-free cloths, such as t-shirts, or good quality cotton swabs.

RUBBER CEMENT
Used whenever a temporary bond is needed, primarily to adhere a leather piece to card stock to prevent stretching and shrinking during tooling.

LEATHER WELD
Used for various applications, such as to attach a lining prior to lacing or stitching.

CONTACT CEMENT
Contact cement is used whenever a permanent bond is required, such as for attaching linings to tooled leatherwork. Good ventilation is a must when using this product, and you should always follow the manufacturer's instructions. Note that water-based cements lack sufficient adhesive strength and durability. Contact cement is available at leathercraft, building supply, woodworking, and hardware stores.

ACRYLIC PAINT

Choosing how to add color to a leather project is another artistic decision the leathercrafter needs to make. By experimenting with the different dyes and paints, you will learn which ones you prefer. Some of the products sold today are available in less-toxic forms for those who are sensitive to fumes or want to be environmentally responsible.

Water-based paints become permanent when dry. They are best used for accent and detailing work rather than overall coloring. They can be used straight out of the bottle or thinned with water to create a wash.

GEL ANTIQUE

Probably the cleanest product to apply, gel antique is thick enough to squirt onto a wool dauber with little mess. It's available in black, dark and medium brown, tan, saddle tan, and mahogany.

LEATHER DYE

A permanent alcohol-based dye that can be applied with a wool dauber or dry sponge. Can be mixed to create different colors or tones.

OIL DYE

Available in black, a range of browns, and several other colors. They penetrate leather deeply and will result in even, highly opaque coverage. They can be applied with a wool dauber or a dry sponge. Latex gloves are recommended to keep the dye from staining your hands.

EDGE KOTE

Protects leather from moisture and imparts a professional finished look. Available in brown and black and is applied with a wool dauber or high-quality cotton swab.

GUM TRAGACANTH

Gum tragacanth comes from the dried root of a legume. When water is added, it becomes a gel. It's the ideal product to help waterproof the flesh side of any unlined leather project. Available at leathercraft supply stores as well as bakery supply stores (it's also used to make cake decorations).

EDGE WAX

Using edge wax to seal the raw edges of belts and other projects is a mark of professionalism. While you can use straight beeswax, many professional leatherworkers use a blend of beeswax and paraffin. It's easy to make and a batch will last for years. Beeswax is available at craft and farm stores; paraffin can be found at most grocery stores.

Making Edge Wax

To make edge wax, you will need equal parts of beeswax and paraffin. An ounce or two of each is plenty. A clean pet food or tuna can is an ideal container for making the wax. Pair it with a plastic pet food can lid and you'll have a convenient storage container. Edge wax can be left out on your work bench or placed in your tool box; it doesn't need to be kept in a sealed container.

The last item you need is a candle warmer or tart burner to melt the wax and paraffin. Alternately, you could melt the waxes on the stove over very low heat using a double boiler. Keep in mind that overheated wax will smoke and catch fire. *Never leave melting wax unattended.*

2. Place the chunks in the can and set the can on the warmer.

1. Place equal parts of paraffin and beeswax on a cutting board. One to two ounces of each will make a long-lasting supply. Use a small kitchen knife to cut the paraffin and beeswax into chunks. Then plug in the candle warmer (or light the candle of the tart burner).

3. It will only take about a half hour for the wax and paraffin to melt and blend together. The actual time will depend on how much product you use. If the mixture does not appear to be fully blended, gently swirl the can or use a craft stick to stir.

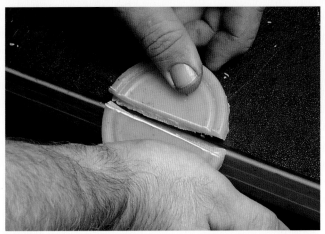

6. Place the disk on the corner of a table and push down on the part that extends over the table to break it.

4. Remove the can from the warmer and let cool. Place in the freezer for an hour or so and the mixture can be easily removal by rapping the can upside down on a hard surface.

7. Use a craft knife to score a shallow line in the center of the two halves.

5. To cut for use, score a shallow line down the center with a utility knife.

8. Line up the scored line with a table edge and push down on the part that extends over the table to break it.

BURNISHING CLOTH

Burnishing the edge of a belt or other project evens out the edge wax, makes two joined pieces of leather look like one, and imparts a warm glow to the leather. One of the best burnishing fabrics is ballistic nylon, a large-weave, shiny, smooth fabric. A good substitute is sports nylon, such as a piece of an old gym bag or an outdoor banner.

LEATHER CONDITIONER

Replaces oils that may have been lost after the leather leaves the tannery and helps preserve leather flexibility and enhance its natural beauty. It also aids in the leather tooling process. Lexol is among the leading brands of leather conditioners.

3-IN-1 BONE FOLDER-CREASER-SLICKER

This multipurpose Craftool is used for edge burnishing and finishing, splitting a sewing seam, applying a guide line, and much more. The head pops off for added versatility. An alternative is a straight bone folder, available at craft stores.

NEATSFOOT OIL

This natural preservative is mostly used on belts, shoes, saddles, and other articles that may be exposed to moisture. It repels water and helps keep leather from drying and cracking. It will also make dried-out leather pliable. May permanently darken light-colored leathers.

LEATHER BALM

Although it does not waterproof leather, this product will add a measure of protection and a warm glow to your leather projects. Apply the neutral color with a clean, soft cloth, let dry, then buff with another clean cloth.

TAN-KOTE

Tan-Kote will provide the same warm non-glossy finish as leather balm but will make your project water-resistant. It's a good choice for work and motorcycle belts that will be exposed to the weather or perspiration.

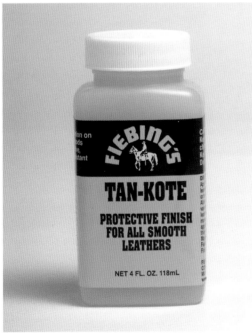

Fasteners and Decorative Elements

Snaps and rivets are available in several sizes. Common colors include nickel, brass, copper, black, and brown. Snaps are not as sturdy as rivets for belts but allow you to switch buckles. Rivets provide a strong, permanent hold and can serve a decorative function as well. Both are applied using similar tools in much the same manner.

SNAPS

A snap-setting kit is made up of four-part snaps, a specially sized setter, and a concave anvil. Snaps come in four parts: a top cap and a bottom female socket, and a rear post and a bottom male socket. Heavy-duty snaps made for 8- to 10-ounce leather are called Line 24 snaps. The setter must be sized to match the size of snap you are using. The anvil is concave to prevent the curved cap from being dented during the application process.

RIVETS

A rivet-setting kit typically comes with a rivet setter and bar anvil along with two-part silver- or brass-colored rivet sets. Rivets are composed of two parts: the top cap, which may be rounded or flat, and the rivet, which has a longer post. They are made of iron or brass coated with a metal alloy finish. Brass-base rivets are preferred; iron-base ones can rust.

Sizing your rivets is important. Select a size that is no more than 2 millimeters (0.08 inch) larger than the width of the two (or more) pieces of leather you are joining. If the rivet post is too short, it will not properly attach the leather pieces. If it is too long, the rivet will tilt and move around in the hole.

The setter has a concave head to prevent marring rounded top caps. The anvil has setting holes to accommodate various sizes of rivets.

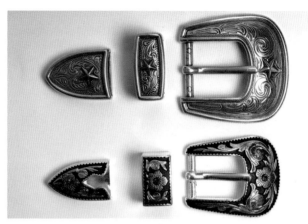

BUCKLES

Once you start your search, you probably will be amazed at the variety of belt buckles that are available. They range in price from a couple of bucks to many hundreds of dollars. Most buckles are made with a standard-sized bar fastened at the base of the buckle (heel bar) or in the center of the buckle (center bar). Regardless of the type, use a leather belt strip that is at least $1/8$ to $1/4$ inch smaller in width than the bar.

CONCHOS

Decorative adornments add personality to your work. They are particularly favored for belts and accessories used by historic reenactors, motorcycle riders, cowboys, and rodeo riders. The inexpensive ones are chrome-, silver-, nickel- or brass-plated metal. Expensive versions are made of brass or sterling silver plate. They are also available in genuine or faux turquoise, mother of pearl, and gemstone. They may have a screw back for easy changing or a rivet back for permanent placement. Slotted types are threaded with lace.

2

Basic Techniques

Now that you are familiar with the various leathercraft tools and supplies, learn how to properly use them. The following step-by-step instructions start with selecting the proper carving and lining leather and end with applying finishing products. Practice these techniques on scrap leather until you feel comfortable with each procedure. And don't be afraid to experiment as you develop your skills, as every leathercrafter's method differs slightly. Once you master these techniques, you'll be able to make the belt and card case covered in chapter 3.

Cowhide Weight Guidelines

Here are general guidelines for selecting leather for specific projects.

Belts: 7- to 8-ounce for 1¹/₂ inches wide,
　　　 9- to 10-ounce for wider belts

Card case: 4- to 5-ounce

Cell phone case: 4- to 5-ounce

Checkbook cover: 4- to 5-ounce

Dog leash: 7- to 8-ounce

Guitar strap: 9- to 10-ounce

Journal and notebook covers: 5- to 6-ounce

Key fob: 4- to 5-ounce

Lining: 2- to 3-ounce

Portable media case: 4- to 5-ounce

Wallets: 4- to 5-ounce

Economy-grade leather is fine for the beginner. Once you gain experience, you can upgrade to the more expensive good and best grades. Purchasing a hide differs from buying fabric. A shoulder or side is priced by the square foot, but you need to choose it based on its intended use. Leathercrafters must take into account the shape of the hide and work around defects, such as soft spots, scars, branding marks, and the like. The leather that is not usable for project pieces can be suitable for carving and stamping practice and colorant testing.

For the demonstration project belt in this book, you'll need a 1¹/₂-inch-wide precut belt strip. For the card case, you'll need a 4- to 6-ounce piece of cowhide about 6 inches square.

Kidskin leather made from a young goat has a shiny appearance, wears well, and is in the higher-price range. It's the best choice to line a card case, wallet, or similar project. You can also use 2-ounce, full-grain, vegetable-tanned cowhide to line your project. This leather may be carefully carved and stamped, unlike other lining options.

Selecting Designs

Master leather toolers render complex patterns, landscapes, and animals in a remarkably realistic way. The beginner should start with simple shapes and borders. A variety of stencils, Craftaids, and patterns allow the novice to get right to tooling. Inspiration can come from almost anywhere: nature, fabric, wallpaper, magazines, catalogs, even a child's coloring book.

Be mindful of using copyrighted material, which often requires written permission to reproduce. The copyright may stipulate that the pattern may be used for personal use only, which means that projects using the patterns may be for your own use or for gifts for family or friends but may not be sold. General ideas for a project, however, are not covered by copyright protection. You can put a rose on a checkbook cover, an eagle on a wallet, or a basket-weave pattern on a belt—just don't use a copyrighted pattern to do so.

Some patterns may be used commercially. Tandy Leather's catalog specifies that Craftaid plastic templates may be used to create leather items for "pleasure, production, or profit." To stay out of trouble, read, understand, and comply with copyrights—and when in doubt, don't use the pattern.

Once you learn the basics of tooling, you will find that design possibilities are boundless. Experiment with different tools and arrange design elements in fresh ways to produce artwork that is uniquely yours.

You are limited only by your imagination when selecting a subject for leather tooling. To transfer a design from the original image to the leather, you will trace it using transfer film or tracing paper. Then transfer the design to wet leather using a stylus tool or ballpoint pen.

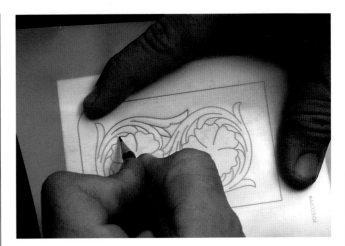

1. Transfer film is used here, but you can use tracing paper, too. Cut your film or paper slightly larger than the design using regular scissors.

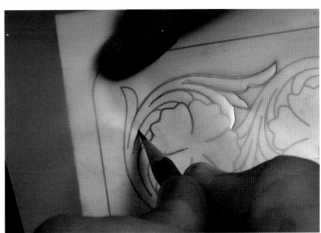

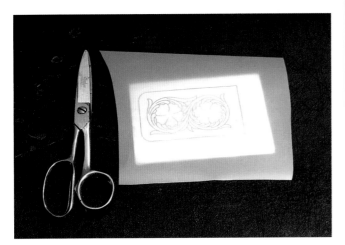

2. It's helpful (though not necessary) to tape your original design on the table and place the film or paper over the original. Tape the film or paper onto the table as well. Experienced tracers hold both down with their free hand.

3. Use a sharp pencil to trace all of the lines on the original design.

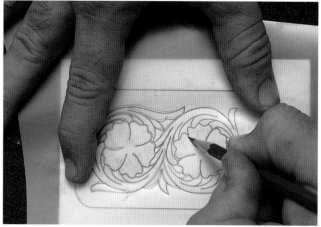

4. A trick to good tracing is to look ahead of the line rather than looking where the pencil point is placed.

5. Be sure you have traced all of the lines

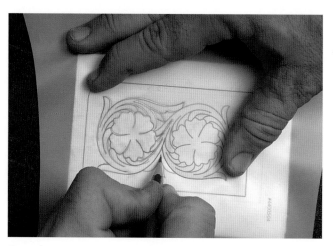

6. If you missed one, replace the film or paper, reregistering it precisely over the original, and complete the tracing.

7. To prevent the oil on your hands from damaging the leather, wash them with dishwashing liquid before making the transfer. With a clean cellulose sponge, wet both sides of the leather with clean water.

8. Spray a moderate amount of leather conditioner (such as Lexol) onto the grain side of the leather.

9. Gently rub the leather conditioner in until it disappears. Do not press hard, to avoid marking the leather.

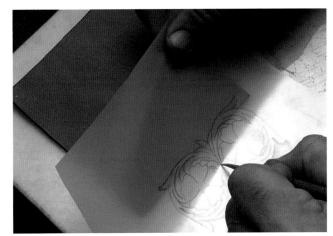

10. First mark the center position of the design on the
leather piece then locate the center of your design on the
film.

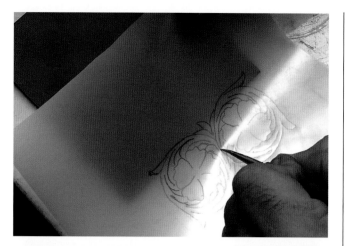

11. Position the film or paper over your leather and match up the center marks.

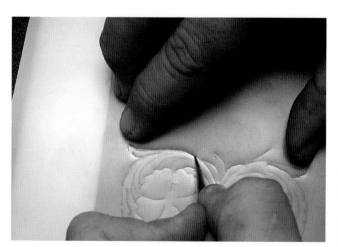

12. Trace the design with the tip of the stylus, pressing hard enough to make an impression but not so hard that you punch through the film or paper.

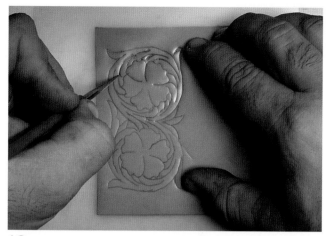

13. Continue tracing until all the lines are transferred onto the leather.

14. Check to make sure you traced all the lines. If not, replace the pattern precisely over the transferred design and complete all lines.

Using a Pattern Template

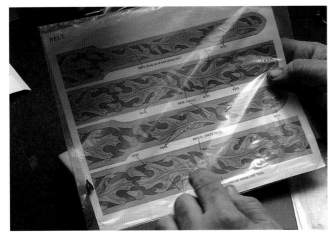

1. Choose the pattern you want to use (one leaf of a Craftaid template is used here).

2. Wet the front and back of your leather. Use your project pattern and mark the center point where the design should be placed on the leather. Locate the center of the portion of the design you wish to use. Match the center marks and adjust the pattern as needed.

3. Slide card stock under the template to mask any portion of the pattern you don't want to transfer.

4. With the spoon end of a stylus tool, or a metal teaspoon, press the lines of the template into the leather.

5. Only moderate pressure is needed to produce clear guidelines. Be sure to transfer all of the lines in the pattern.

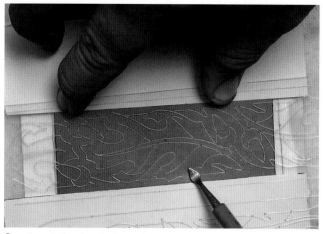

6. Carefully check the edges of the pattern to be sure you are not pressing on any lines you do not want. Remember that the guidelines will be permanently embossed on the leather.

8. If you missed some lines, replace the template, re-register the lines, and complete the transfer.

7. Check your design to make sure you transferred all the lines by careful lifting the template up on one side.

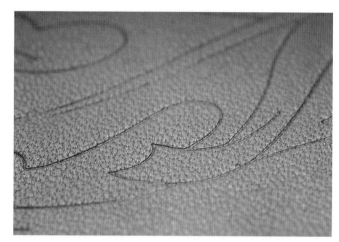

9. The plastic template does a good job of producing easy-to-see guidelines. Your design is now ready to be carved and stamped.

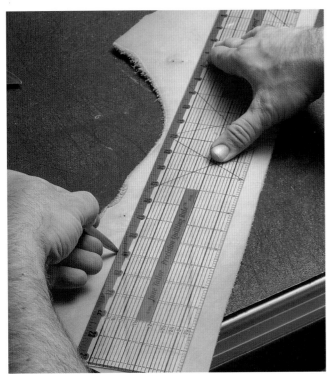

1. To make a straight cut, you can use a utility knife. Position a transparent ruler or L square on the grain side of a piece of leather where you want to cut. Use a pen or pencil to draw a line along the length of the rule.

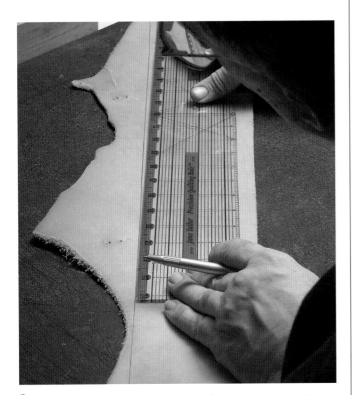

2. Keep the straight edge on your line as you move it several inches at a time to continue marking a straight line. Do this until you reach the end of the hide.

3. Hold the straight edge down firmly with one hand and place the blade of a utility knife at the beginning of the line at a 90-degree angle to the line.

4. Apply even pressure and start cutting the leather by pulling the knife toward you, going about 5 or 6 inches with each pull. Carefully reposition the hand holding down the leather so it is close to where you are cutting. Try to keep the knife at a 90-degree angle as you cut.

Keep the utility knife below the hand that holds it at all times so that if the knife slips, you won't cut yourself. Beginners may find it easier to use an L square that has a thicker edge, making it easier to keep the knife against the straight edge.

Here, the blade was not held against the straight edge throughout the entire cut. The entire edge should be re-marked about $1/4$ inch in from the original line and the hide should be re-cut.

5. Uneven pressure or a dull blade will result in spurs. Use your utility knife to clean up the edge.

Using a Round Knife

1. This tool can cut straight and curved lines and is a key part of the experienced leathercrafter's tool kit. To use it, grip the knife tightly close to the blade with the thumb pressing on the handle. Place the blade tip closest to you at the beginning of the cut.

2. Hold the blade at a 90-degree angle so the cut edge is straight. Roll the blade forward on your guideline. Keep your free hand well away from the blade.

3. Lift the blade then re-set the tip where you left off.

4. Repeat the cutting process by rolling the blade forward.

5. Don't be concerned if the end of the leather curls toward you or portions start to buckle. Concentrate only on the area you are cutting.

6. When you reach the end, roll the knife off the leather onto your cutting surface.

Using a Rotary Cutter

Seamstresses and quilters are fond of this tool, as it will cut through several layers of fabric with one pass and is easily maneuvered on curves. A heavy-duty model is a must for leathercrafters. It is best suited for use on lining leather and lightweight tooling leathers, but it will cut through a heavier 8- to 10-ounce vegetable-tanned piece of tooling leather.

   To use a rotary cutter, hold the handle firmly and roll the blade along the straight edge using even downward pressure along the entire length of the leather you are cutting. Move the straight edge as needed to reach the end of the line. On heavy leather, you may need to repeat the process several times until you cut completely through the leather. Blades must be sharp, so have spares on hand.

Using a Skiver

1. The skiver is used on dry leather. Sharp blades make the job go easier, so have spares on hand. A skiver removes up to half the thickness of a piece of leather so that it doesn't crack when folded. Leather is skived from the flesh side in small areas, a little at a time.

Basic Techniques

2. Grip the skiver near the neck with your thumb or first finger resting on the handle. Place the skiver blade on the leather and, with medium pressure, pull back and up. Don't skive in the same direction with every stroke. Rotate the blade to evenly remove leather.

3. For small pieces, such as this belt keeper, it is easier to place the piece at the edge of your table (on your cutting surface) and skive downward off the table.

Artists have used hand tools to decorate leather goods for centuries. Carving leather refers to using a swivel knife to carve basic shapes into the leather and using stamps to give the object a three-dimensional and detailed appearance.

Tooling also encompasses stamping patterns without initial carving. An infinite number of designs can be created with the stamps available today.

The following oak leaf tutorial demonstrates the basics of carving and stamping.

1. When thin leather is wet, it has a tendency to stretch out of shape when stamped. To prevent this, use rubber cement to adhere the leather to a piece of poster board or heavy card stock. Note that this technique is used on 4- to 6-ounce cowhide and not on belts, which are made from heavier 6- to 8-ounce hide.

2. Start with a piece of cowhide cut to the size of your project. Cut a piece of card stock slightly larger than the leather. Trace the outline of the project onto the paper.

3. Brush rubber cement on the paper only—not the leather—within the lines.

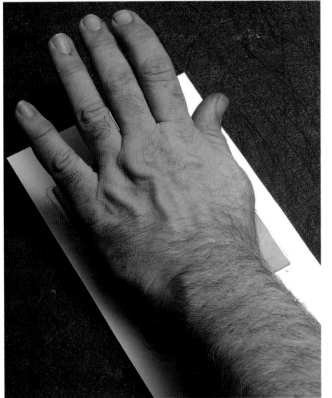

4. Be careful not to get rubber cement of the grain side of the leather. Place the leather flesh-side down on the rubber-cemented area of the card. Press down firmly to adhere. Place a stone block or other heavy object over the piece and let it dry overnight.

Note that leather heavier than 6 ounces is typically not glued for tooling: It's not an exact science, so when in doubt, it's best to glue it down.

Carving with a Swivel Knife

The swivel knife is used to cut the primary lines of your design. These lines are then beveled to make the design three-dimensional. This is enhanced by stamping the area around the design with a background tool, and the object can be further embellished with various other stamps.

Design patterns you purchase should come with instructions that will show which lines to carve, making it easier for the beginner. Once you complete a few tooling projects, you will understand the process and should not hesitate to carve a design unaided by a guide.

Practice and experience will enable you to become an expert carver. Remember, leather tooling is an art and need not be perfect. Most "mistakes" can be corrected, and chances are only you will notice minor flaws.

Just as determining the proper wetness of the leather is a matter of experience, so is determining the depth of a cut. The cuts need to be deep and aggressive, but smooth. Some carvers will say the depth of the carving should be a specific proportion of the thickness of the leather, but there is no firm rule.

General Rules of Carving

- Carve with the leather piece on the smooth side of your stone block.
- Never carve on dry leather.
- Leather conditioner makes the leather claylike and easier to carve.
- Strop your blade every time you put the knife down and pick it up again.
- Strop your blade if it starts to drag while making a cut.
- Strive to consistently cut through the leather at the same depth.
- Carve your lines from the inside of your design toward the outside. This will keep you from squashing the lines you already made.
- Don't allow lines to intersect. Leave a tiny space of leather between lines.
- Be more concerned about cutting smoothly rather than following the lines exactly.

1. You'll get the best results from your swivel knife work if you strop it every time you pick it up and when it starts to drag. First apply a generous amount of white jeweler's rouge onto the strop surface.

2. Place the swivel knife blade on the strop and pull it toward you with the bevel of the blade held flat against the strop.

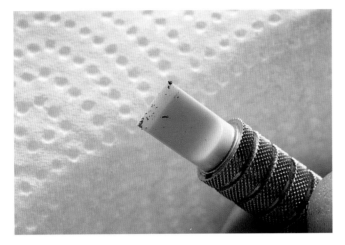

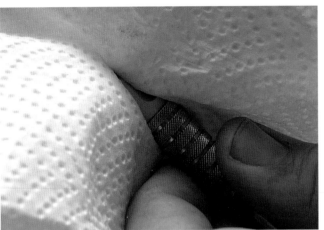

3. Use a paper towel or cloth to remove the dirt and residue the blade might have picked up.

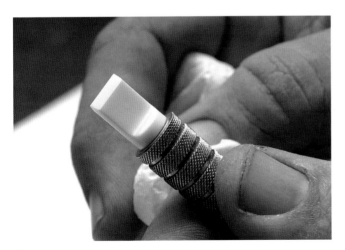

4. The blade is clean and ready to cut.

The Tooling Process

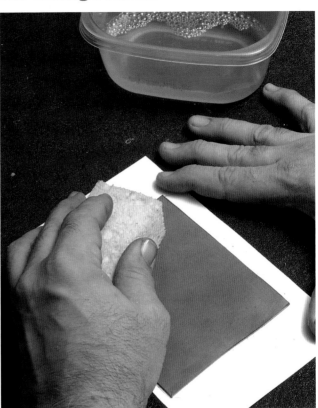

1. Use clean water and a clean sponge to wet the entire surface of the leather on both sides.

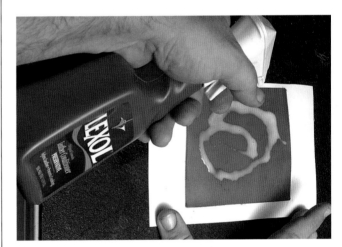

2. Spray on a generous amount of leather conditioner.

3. Gently rub in the leather conditioner in a circular motion using your fingers until it is all absorbed. Then transfer the design to the leather as described on pages 27–32.

4. Once your leather is at the proper moisture level, you're ready to carve. A ceramic blade is used here. It's okay if your blade is metal: The procedure is exactly the same, and, if you carve properly, you will achieve the same results.

Hold the swivel knife by placing your forefinger in the yoke. Place your thumb and middle fingers on the knurled areas. These two fingers control the swivel action of the blade. Your little finger rides lightly on the leather as you make your cuts.

Oak Leaf Pattern

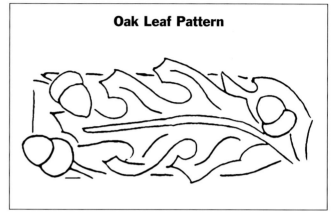

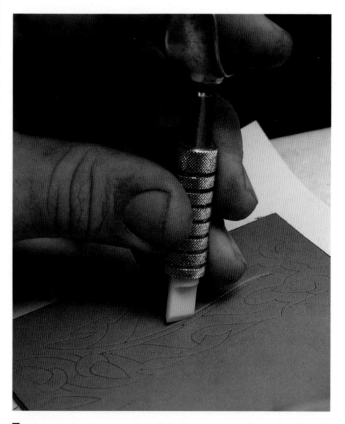

5. Insert the corner of the blade on an angle at the tip of a line.

- Whether you are making designs using a stamp or using the swivel knife to make decorative cuts, the leather you are working on must be wet. Wet leather is very delicate so be careful not to drop any tools or liquids on your piece.

- Water is applied to the leather using a clean sponge on both the grain and flesh sides of the piece. This is called "casing the leather." About 80 percent of the water should be applied to the flesh side and only 20 percent to the grain side. After this initial wetting, water should be applied as needed to the flesh side only.

- Never spot-wet leather or you risk making permanent stains. If you take a break from tooling and your leather dries out, re-wet the entire piece before you resume work.

- After you first wet the leather, you must wait for a short time for the leather to dry a bit. Carving on too-wet or too-dry leather results in lines that are not even, crisp, and clean. The blade will tend to sink in too far on too-wet leather and drag on too-dry leather. Stamps will penetrate too deeply and leave a sloppy impression on too-wet leather or a weak impression on too-dry leather.

- Determining the drying time is more of an art than a science and comes only with practice. Observe the color of the leather before you begin and after you wet it. The perfect color for tooling is right in between those shades. If in doubt, it's better to err on the dry side.

- Check for proper wetness by placing the back of your hand on the leather. It should feel cool to the touch.

- The tooling process demonstrated here includes an application of leather conditioner after wetting. This helps give the leather a claylike consistency, which results in easier carving and stamping and better results.

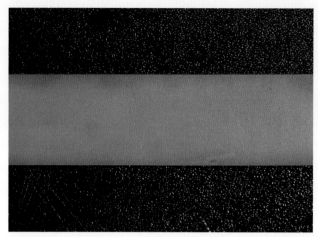

Too dry for tooling

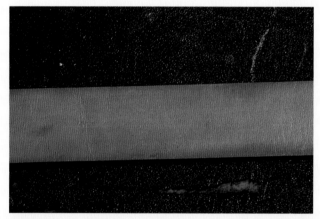

Too wet for tooling

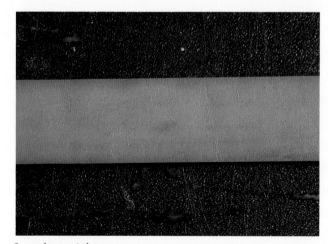

Just about right

Basic Techniques

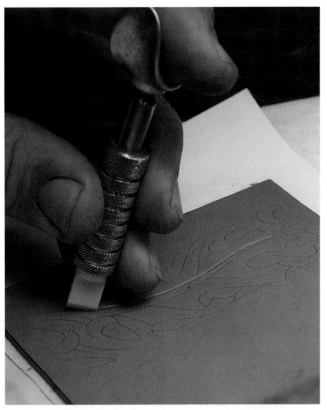

6. Tilt the blade forward slightly and press into the leather. Use an even downward pressure on the blade while pulling it toward you in one smooth motion.

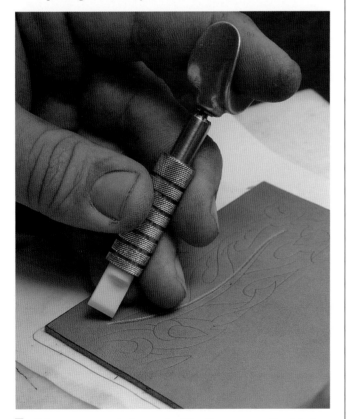

7. When you reach the end of the line, swoop the blade out of the leather. Remember, cutting with a smooth, continuous motion is more important than following the line exactly.

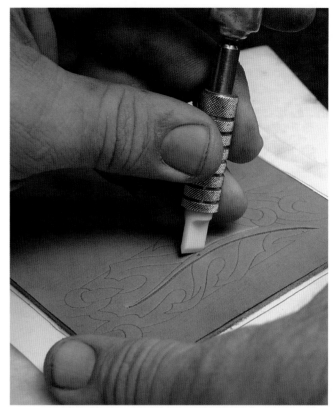

8. Carve your pattern from the inside to the outside of the design. With this oak leaf, the main vein is carved first.

9. The vein lines should be completed in one continuous motion without lifting the blade.

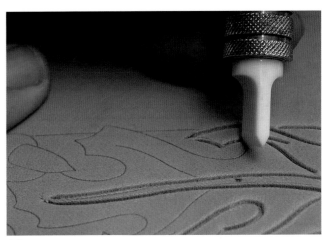

12. Curved lines are the most difficult to master because you need to use the swivel feature of the blade to make the curve in one continuous cut. Start by inserting the corner of your blade at the top of the curved line.

10. Instead of stopping at the end and lifting, swoop the blade out.

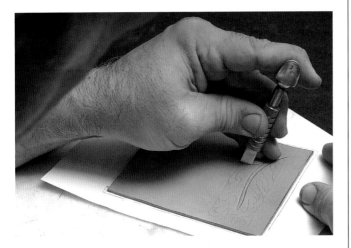

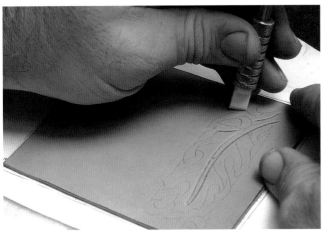

11. The same technique is used to carve the short secondary leaf veins in the design.

13. With even, downward pressure, pull the knife toward you, swiveling the blade with your thumb and middle fingers as you go around the curve.

14. Swoop the blade out at the end of the cut.

15. This is how the curved cut should look.

16. This is how the whole design appears at this point. Note that no carved lines intersect.

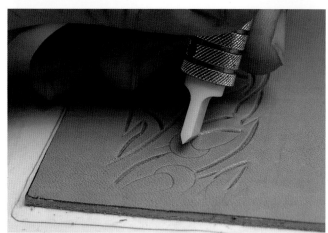

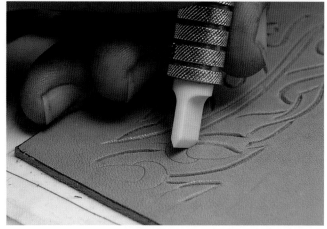

17. Round shapes, such as the acorn, are completed in two steps. Place the corner of the knife blade at the top of one side. In one smooth stroke, pull the knife toward you and swoop out where the line starts to curve.

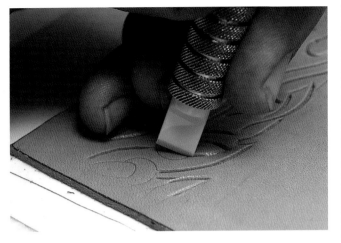

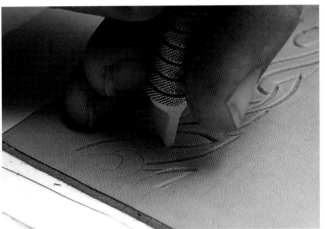

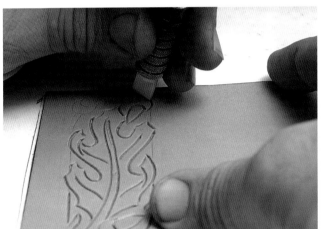

18. Place your blade at the tip of the acorn again and cut the second side of the acorn, but this time continue your cut around the base of the nut. If you find it easier to cut a curve one way or another—to the left or the right—simply turn your work upside down.

19. The cap of the acorn is carved in one complete stroke. Place the corner of your blade at the beginning of one end of the cap. (Carve the curve from the side that is most comfortable for you.) Use the tool's swivel action to curve around the arc and stop at the end of the line.

47

20. Carve the other acorn and the edge lines at the top and bottom. Note that some of the design lines on the right and left are being left uncarved. You will see how this treatment works once the piece is stamped.

Making Final Decorative Cuts

1. Fine decorative cuts are made after the stamping is complete. These smooth curvy cuts add visual interest to the design.

Sign Your Work

These days, almost everything is factory-made, so a handmade item is relatively rare and special. Your handmade leather piece is one-of-a-kind, even if you use a project and/or design pattern. Your time and talent deserves to be recognized with a signature.

Some leathercraft suppliers sell three-dimensional stamping tools that include the words "Handcrafted by." You can either use your swivel knife to carve your initials or alphabet stamps to finish the phrase. Or you can develop your own signature mark. Either way, your signed leather pieces will become treasured gifts or heirlooms.

Add your name or initials to a three-dimensional stamp.

Create your own signature mark using your swivel knife.

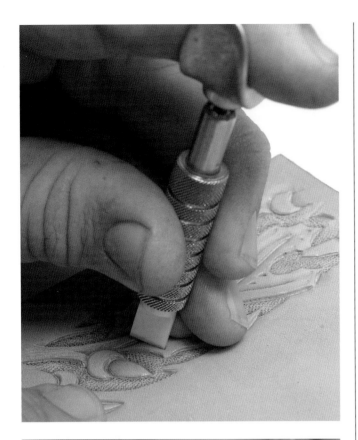

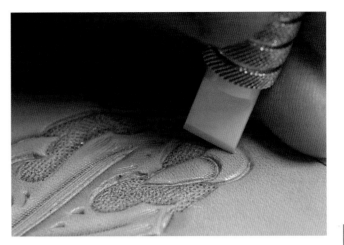

3. The crosshatch pattern in the acorn caps is made very lightly.

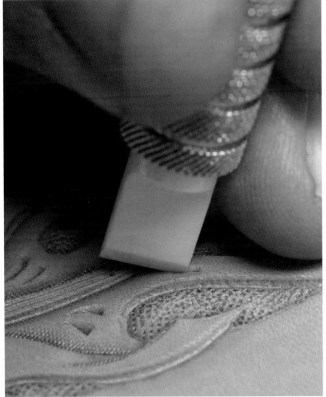

2. Detail cuts are made by plunging the knife tip into the leather, making a short stroke, and removing the knife with a swift swoop.

4. Decorative cuts sometimes violate the no-intersecting-lines rule. Notice that you need only to suggest the pattern in the acorn cap. You don't need to overdo the crosshatch lines to create a realistic look. Also note how the decorative leaf cuts are broader where the knife was first plunged in.

Once your design is carved, put your creativity to work by enhancing the design with tooling stamps. This section shows the purposes of the stamping tools used most in design work and how to use them.

1. The first step in stamping is to test your leather for the proper moisture content. If it is too dry, rewet it and wait until it is ready. Unless otherwise noted, all tools should be held vertically with the thumb and forefinger. Often, leather toolers will rest their little finger lightly on the project piece.

Basic Rules of Stamping

- Use the smooth side of your stone block for stamping.

- Never stamp on dry leather.

- If you tend to pound the stamp too hard, try choking up on the mallet by holding the handle closer to the mallet head.

2. The beveling tool is one of the only stamping tools that should be stropped. Rub the face and sides of the tool across the strop before use and periodically while stamping. This will ensure a smooth movement across the leather, resulting in a nicely beveled edge.

3. With some exceptions, most stamping tools are struck lightly two or three times with the tool held vertically.

Remember: If your leather dries out too much while you are working (if the swivel knife drags or stamp impressions are too light), rewet the entire piece of leather, not just a portion. If a piece is not finished in one sitting, rewet the entire piece of leather before you begin again.

Beveling

Beveling is the single most important process in creating three-dimensional leatherwork. The goal of using this tool is to free the figure from the background. The beveling tool is placed next to a cut edge and is used to compress the leather. To achieve the 3-D effect, you must bevel only one side of a line.

Bevelers come in many widths and can have a smooth-finish head or a textured head. Leather is always beveled first with the smooth-finish tool and beveled a second time with the textured beveler if more detail is desired.

To bevel a carved line, you place the flat edge of the beveler on the cut. Lightly tap the tool multiple times while moving it along the line.

1. The beveler used here is Craftool B-203. Place the flat side of the beveling tool against the outside of the vein line.

51

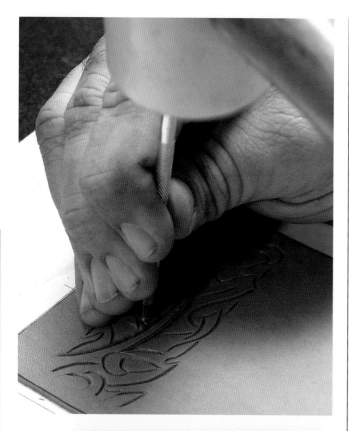

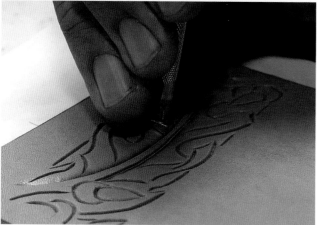

2. Keep the beveler tool moving smoothly along the line as you gently tap with the mallet as you go. Generally, the tool is moved about half of its width with each tap. Hold the tool loosely and allow the tool to bounce as you go along.

3. Continue tapping and moving the beveler until you come to the end of the vein. If the tool starts to drag, strop it. As with carving, you want to bevel the figures from the center of the design outward to the edges.

4. You should not see any individual tool marks along the beveled cut. If you can see tool marks or want the vein to stand out more, rebevel the cut. Bevel the other side of the vein on the outside so that the entire vein is lifted off the leather.

5. You'll bevel all of the smaller veins on the same side of the cut line. Notice the darker color produced by the beveler. This indicates that there is proper moisture content in the leather.

6. You'll bevel all of the leaf parts along the outside edges.

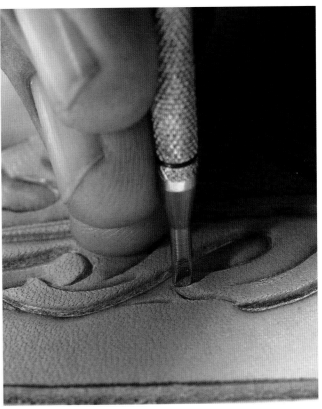

7. Switch to a smaller smooth-faced beveler to bevel tight spots. Here, Craftool B935 is used. Take your time when beveling curves in tight areas. Notice how high the leaf has been raised over the background—the goal of beveling.

8. Notice the difference beveling has made on the upper side of the oak leaf.

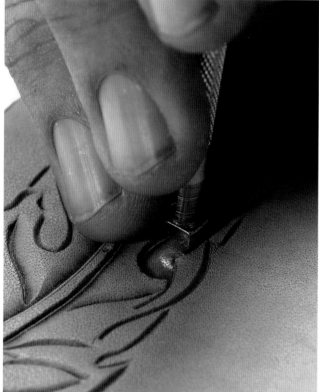

9. You'll continue beveling the entire leaf and acorn out-lines. Check your work before moving on to ensure that you didn't miss any lines.

Adding a Background

Basic backgrounds are usually made with one of the many crosshatch or matte tools, but you will find some fanciful work that uses flower shapes, too.

A background adds focus to your main carving figures.

The face of the background tool is small and care must be taken not to strike the tool too hard. It's also important that the impressions are evenly spaced and the entire background area is stamped.

The tool can be angled to get into small spaces.

1. The background tool is held at a 90-degree angle and tapped with the mallet one or two times. To make light, controlled taps, hold the mallet close to the head.

2. Then lift up the tool and move it to an adjacent area. The tool used here is Craftool A104.

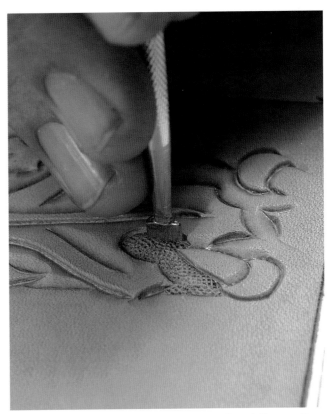

3. Turn the head of the background tool in different directions as you go.

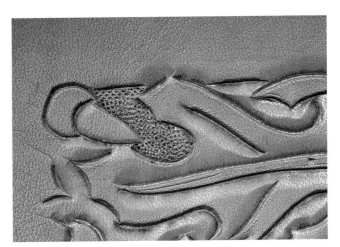

4. Stamping should be of even depth and not overlapped, though some overlapping is inevitable. When dyed, the background will appear to be much darker.

Basic Techniques

55

5. Take care to stay within the carved lines of the outside border.

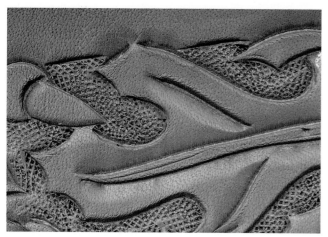

6. The goal of a good background is to appear inconspicuous. Its purpose is to draw attention to the main figures.

USING A BALL END MODELING TOOL

This tool is used to make hard edges round and smooth. By rounding the edges, you accentuate the three-dimensional effect of carving and beveling. Use a gentle hand with this tool so you don't depress the beveled edge.

1. Run the ball tip along the leaf veins to make them appear to have rounded edges

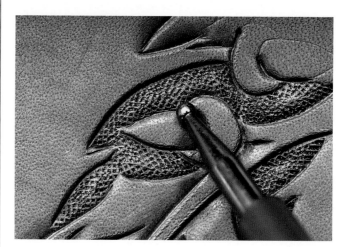

2. The modeling tool also helps make these acorns appear to have a curved shape.

USING A PEAR SHADER

A pear shader makes a design element, such as a flower petal or leaf, appear curved. It has either a smooth or textured face. The tool can be held at a 90-degree angle or tilted to fit into a tight area and can be "walked" across an area as it is tapped for even coverage.

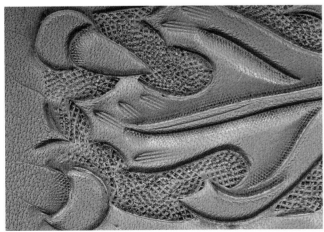

In this instance, just the tip of the shader is used to add dimension to the leaf tips. Be sure to position the tool exactly where you want it. Hold the tool at a 90-degree angle and tap one or two times with the mallet.

USING A TEXTURE BEVELER

1. A texture beveler is used to add more dimension and interest to the oak leaf center vein. Unlike other stamping tools used in this project, the texture beveler is used alone, without a mallet.

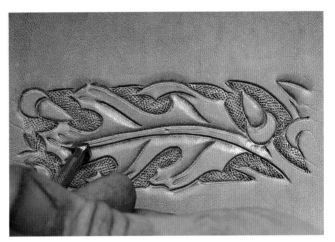

2. Hold the tool at a 90-degree angle and run it down the stem in a continuous movement with moderate to heavy pressure.

3. Follow the line of the vein, keeping the tool centered between the edges.

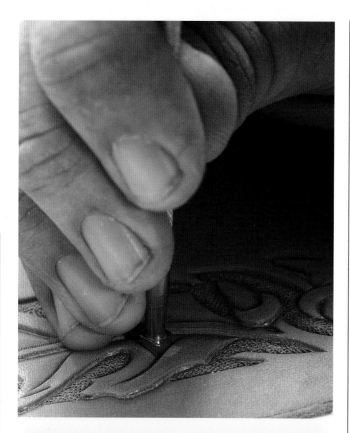

To detail the area beveled with a smooth beveler, you may wish to go over it again with the texture beveler to add more interest and dimension to the work. Here we wanted to emphasize the leaf veins. The texture beveler is used in the same manner as the smooth beveler. The goal is to make a smooth bevel with no visible tool marks.

OTHER TOOLS

Seeder, veiner, and camouflage tools are used extensively in western floral tooling. They are also effective design elements in borders.

The seeder tool is often used to represent seeds. Impressions are made at the same depth and should not be overlapped. Care should be taken not to strike this tool too hard as it could go right through the leather. The tool is held at a 90-degree angle and tapped lightly with the mallet.

The camouflage tool adds interest to leaves and flowers. It is held at a 90-degree angle to make evenly spaced (not overlapped) impressions.

The veiner tool makes a curved line impression and is used to make an object, such as a leaf, appear to be curved. To achieve this, the tool is often tilted so that the impression is deeper and darker on one side. There are many veiner tool designs in curve sizes from just under $1/2$ inch to $1^1/4$ inches.

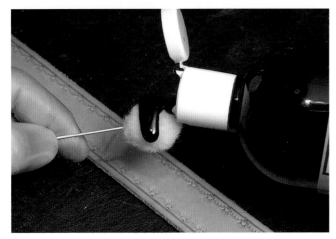

1. Water-based antique gels impart a rich color and a polished luster to leather projects. The gels are easy to apply. The project you are dying should be dry. Start by applying a moderate amount of gel to a wool dauber or a clean, lint-free cloth.

2. Apply a generous amount to dye the entire grain surface. If you are working on a project that will not be lined, dye the flesh side, as well.

3. Reapply gel to the dauber or cloth as needed.

4. Be sure to dye all exposed edges of the piece, regardless of whether they will show after final assembly.

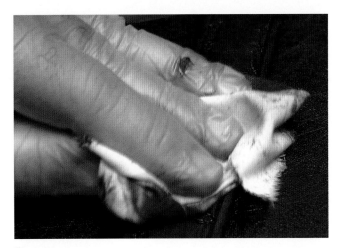

5. As soon as you are finished applying the gel, use a clean lint-free cloth to rub the gel into the leather and remove the excess.

TIP: Stained projects should be left to dry for 24 hours before any other work is done or final finish is applied.

6. Don't be concerned if you see a bit of color variance. Some striations can be expected.

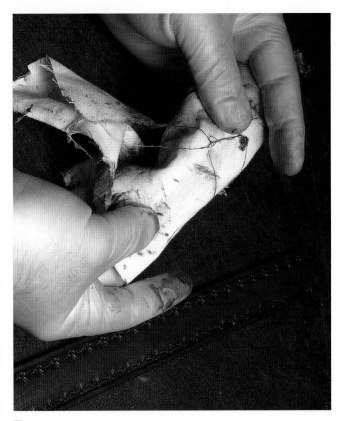

7. Keep turning your cloth as it becomes saturated with dye to expose a clean area.

8. Continue rubbing the gel into the leather until there is no raw leather showing.

9. Don't be stingy with the amount of gel you use. Use the wool dauber to really work the color into the stamped areas. Then rub with a cloth and check to see that the stain has penetrated the leather.

10. The trickiest part of staining a stamped leather piece is ensuring that the gel penetrates all crevices. A close-up inspection shows two areas that were missed in the process. Misapplied colorant can be corrected by restaining the item, as antique stain is very forgiving. You can restain only the areas that require it, rather than the entire piece.

Using Antique Gel with Dye as an Accent Color

1. Use a good quality paintbrush for precise application. Here the red dye is applied along a stamping guideline and on both edges of a belt. Take time to ensure that the dye is applied evenly and completely.

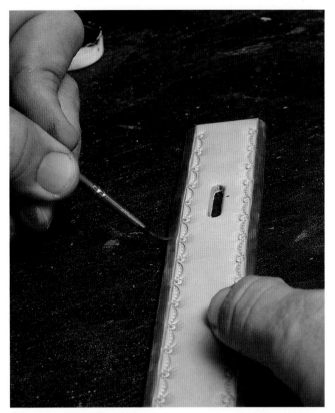

2. A second coat may be applied right away if you want the color to be darker.

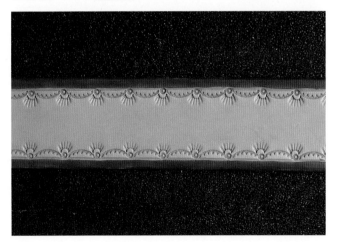

3. Let the dye dry overnight before apply antique gel stain to the center of the belt.

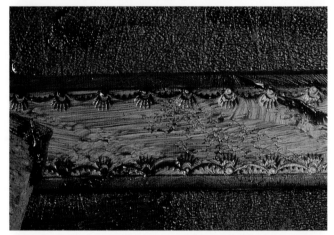

4. The easiest way to color the center of the belt is to apply an all-over coat of antique gel. Light brown was used here. Use a slightly damp sponge or a wool dauber to apply the gel.

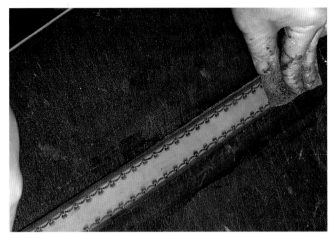

5. Depending on what color you use, the gel stain may slightly darken other dyed areas, such as the red edge. If the antique gel color isn't dark enough to suit you, reapply while the leather is still damp.

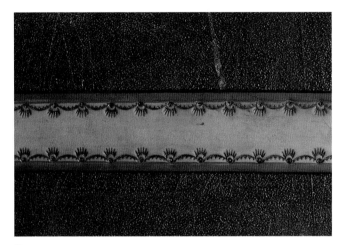

6. Gel stain enhances the stamping pattern by making it darker than the surrounding leather. Streaks or dark marks are caused by imperfections and striations in the leather and are unavoidable.

Note: If you were to use dye instead of the antique gel stain, you would not be able to apply it over previously dyed areas. In this example, dye would drastically darken the red edge or it would overdye it completely, depending on the dye color used.

Acrylic Paint

Acrylic paints can be used to highlight a three-dimensional stamp, edge a border, or color large areas. These water-based paints may be thinned to create a wash or combined with other colors to make new ones.

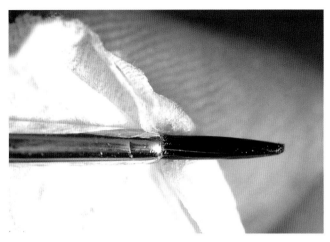

1. Select the proper size brush to suit the area you are painting. For detail work, use a fairly good quality liner or script brush to apply acrylic paints.

2. If you are doing fine work, dip the brush in water and use your fingers to sharpen the point of the brush.

3. Pour, dip, or squirt a small amount of paint on a piece of cardstock or paper plate.

4. Thin the paint if it is too thick for a smooth application.

5. Carefully apply the paint. Should you brush or splatter some where you don't want it, wipe it off immediately with a damp cloth.

6. Acrylic paints dry quickly and are waterproof when dry.

The leather disk in this holiday ornament was dyed and then detailed with acrylic paint.

Leather and Oil Dyes

Alcohol-based leather dye and oil dye are permanent and come in a wide range of colors. Oil dye is touted as offering better coverage and being more colorfast that alcohol-based dye. Latex gloves are recommended while applying these, as they will stain your hands.

The easiest way to apply dye is to dip the entire piece into a dye-filled bowl or pan until the dye is evenly absorbed and then leave it to dry for several days on newspapers or an old towel. As with all colorants, it's a good idea to test your color on a scrap piece of leather before dyeing your project.

If your piece is too large to dip or you want to use more than one color on your project, use a wool dauber to apply the dye completely and evenly. Dyes are usually used for an all-over application, but they can be applied decoratively to select areas.

Remember that if you use dye instead of antique gel, you must keep the colors separate. Dye is very opaque and will darken, change, or obliterate any previously applied colors.

Basic Techniques

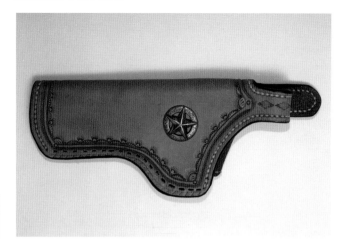

1. You might not want to color your project at all. By applying neatsfoot oil, you can achieve a warm, natural appearance without dyes. The most efficient way to apply this oil is by dipping leather into it.

Basic Techniques

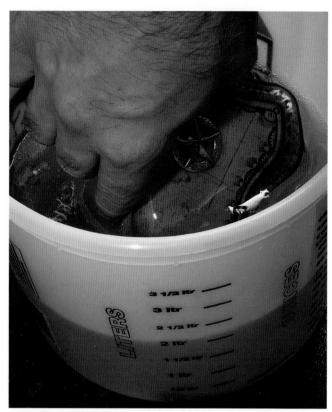

3. Submerge the item fully. Neatsfoot oil will not harm your skin, so gloves are not necessary.

2. Fill a container large enough to hold your item with an ample amount of oil so the item can be dipped.

4. Continue to dip the item until it is completely covered. The used oil can be returned to its original container for reuse; the bucket can be cleaned with soap and water.

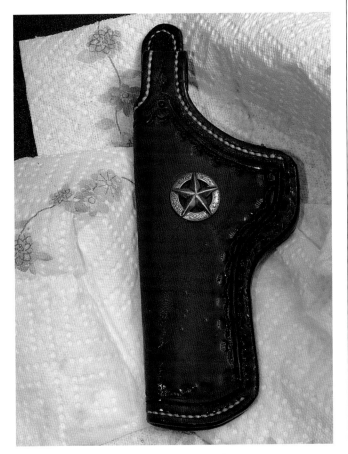

5. Towel off the item so it no longer drips.

6. Hang the item over a paper towel or set it the edge of the bucket to dry for several days.

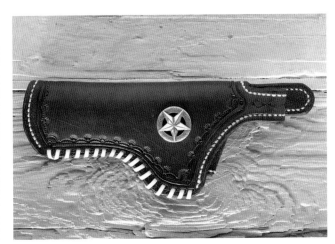

7. The neatsfoot oil will darken the leather, giving it a subtly colored appearance. The oil will help repel water and keep the leather from drying out and cracking.

Attaching fasteners isn't difficult, but it does take practice and proper technique. If you don't tap the fastener hard enough, it won't stay put. If you tap it too hard, you risk damaging it.

Here are some good tips to follow:

- Select the proper size snap or rivet for the job (as described on page 24).

- Practice on a similar weight scrap leather before working on your project. It's worth sacrificing a few snaps or rivets.

- Keep your tool at a 90-degree angle when initially setting the snap or rivet.

- Double check to make sure the parts are oriented properly.

- Many light taps are far better than one or two crushing blows. Taps should be given "around the clock" from all directions as you tip the tool.

1. First match up your snap parts: the cap attaches to the female socket, and the rear rivet attaches to the male socket. Then select the anvil hole that is the same size as the cap.

2. Make sure the snap handle is the proper size. The handle prong should fit snugly in the female socket.

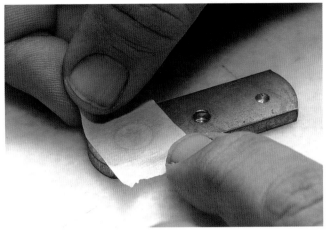

3. Prepare the anvil by placing a piece of masking tape over the correct anvil depression to prevent it from marring the surface of your snap cap.

4. Push the stem of the female socket from the flesh side through the snap hole to the grain side.

5. Place the cap on the anvil and insert the female socket.

6. Place the setting handle at a 90-degree angle. Make one or two strong taps to set the snap, and then tap lightly while moving the top of the handle in a circular motion to secure the top to the bottom.

Basic Techniques

7. The cap and the female socket are in place.

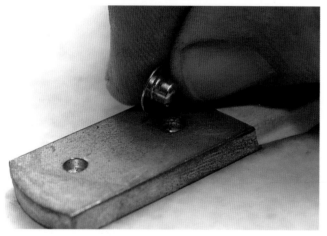

8. To set the bottom set of snap parts, place the male socket in the proper anvil hole.

9. Place the male rear rivet through the grain side to the flesh side of the leather.

10. Press the two pieces together until you hear a snap.

12. As before, place the snap setter handle on the snap at a 90-degree angle. Make one or two moderate taps. Then make additional light taps while moving the top of the handle in a circular motion to secure all sides of the snap.

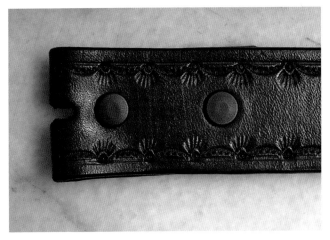

Rivets are set in the same manner as snaps, except there are only two parts: the cap and post.

Attaching Rivets

Here are a nickel and a brass set of rivets. The male posts are at the top and the caps are below.

1. Refer to page 24 for information on sizing your rivets properly.

2. Line up the holes in both pieces of leather you are attaching and insert the post. Be sure you are orienting your cap and post properly.

3. Place the post in the cap and use your fingers to press the two parts together.

4. Place the rivet cap top-side-down in the proper anvil hole. (If your rivet cap is rounded, use a circular concave anvil.)

5. Make a series of small taps until the rivet is properly set.

Stitching Leather

1. Tools you will need to saddle stitch include waxed linen thread in the color of your choice, two stitching needles, and a stitching awl with a trapezoidal needle. You also need a stitching groover and a stitching wheel. (A stitching wheel is used here.) A stitching pony holds your project while you use both hands to punch thread holes and manipulate two needles to sew the leather pieces together.

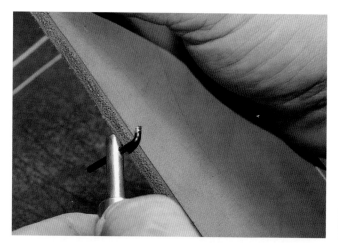

2. As a general rule, stitching lines should be as far from the edge of the piece as the leather is thick. Set the width on your stitching groover by inserting a strip of the same leather thickness you are using for your project.

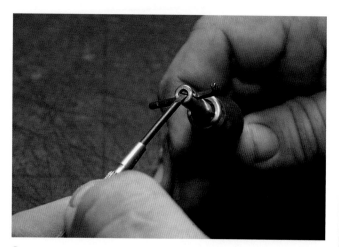

3. Use a small screwdriver to secure the bar loosely.

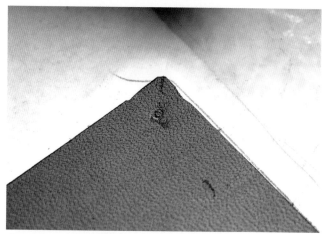

4. Using the stitching groover, make marks where the two grooves coming into a corner will meet. Repeat for the other three corners.

5. Place the groover tip on one of the marks you just made. Hold your project down with one hand and, with the other, pull the groover toward you. The shaft of the groover tool rides along the edge of the leather. Pull with moderate pressure. Stop when you reach the corner mark.

6. Repeat this process on all edges you want to stitch. (Only three edges have been grooved here.)

7. Use the groover tool to deepen the cut by going over each groove a second time.

8. To make the stitching-hole indicator marks, place one of the points of the overstitch wheel in a corner hole.

9. With firm, even pressure, run the tool along each edge, being careful to keep the tool in the groove.

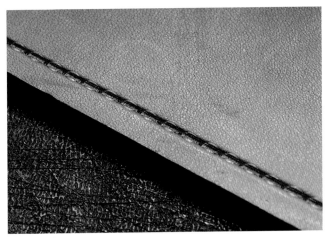

10. Here is how the stitch marks should look. Stop at each corner and place one of the points in the corner hole to mark the next groove.

11. Go over the groove again to deepen the stitching hole indicator marks. Make sure you realign the tool points in the stitching holes you just made.

Working With Thread

Determine the maximum amount of thread you can work with by holding one end of thread in one hand and the spool in the other. Extend one hand out as far as you can reach. Double this length and cut the thread off the spool. (As a general rule, lengths over 6 feet are hard to handle.)

Note: If you run low on thread while stitching your project, you can splice in additional thread (the splicing technique is illustrated on page 84).

1. Insert the tip of the thread through one of the needles. It may help to flatten the tip by pressing it between your fingers. Leave about a 2-inch tail extending from the end of the needle.

3. Push the point of the needle all the way through the thread.

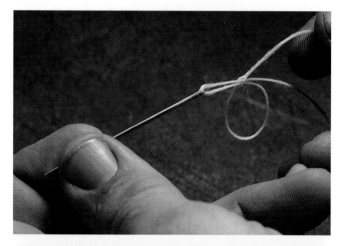

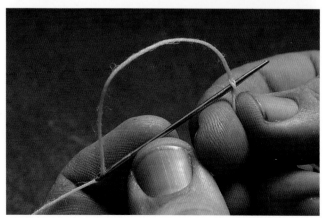

2. You are now going to pierce the thread several inches away from the needle to form a straight line knot.

Basic Techniques

4. Hold the short and long ends of the thread and pull the needle all of the way through the thread. When you pull the thread taut, it will form a knot at the base of the needle.

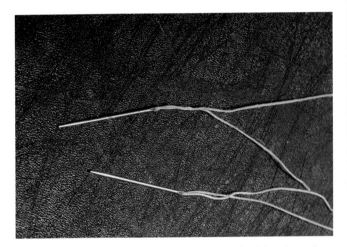

5. Repeat the process with the other end of the thread and the second needle.

6. Set aside your needles, being careful not to tangle the threads, while you set your project in the stitching pony.

7. Place your project—here we're using a card case—between the jaws of the stitching pony with the stitching line about 1/4 inch above the wood post. Secure firmly by tightening the wing nuts.

8. Use the stitching awl with the 2 blade to punch the first hole in the corner mark made by the stitching wheel. All punching is done from the front side of the item.

9. Punch the entire needle through the leather up to the tool's hilt.

Orienting your awl blade properly

Correct: This diagram shows the proper orientation of the punch awl blade within the stitching groove when making stitching holes.

Incorrect: This diagram illustrates punches that were made above and below the stitching groove and with the blade tilted at various angles.

10. The punch awl blade is in the shape of a parallelogram. It is very important that you maintain the correct orientation of the blade with every punch and to stay within the stitching groove.

11. Continue punching on the hole marks. Be sure to keep your fingers clear of the awl blade. Continue punching until you reach the end of the stitching pony arm.

12. Pick up your needles and insert one in the corner hole. Pull the thread through until half of the thread is on either side.

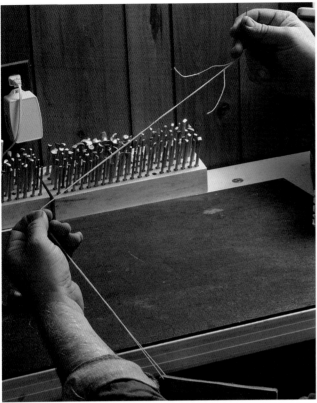

13. Put both needles in one hand and extend you arm to check that the thread is of equal length on both sides. Adjust if necessary.

Note: A piece of tooling leather cut to the diameter of the hilt will prevent the tool from making marks on your leather piece as you are making the stitching holes. After cutting out the proper size circle, mark the center and punch through using the stitching awl.

14. Place the front-side needle through the second hole from front to back and pull it through.

77

15. With the other needle, go through from the back side into the same hole you just used.

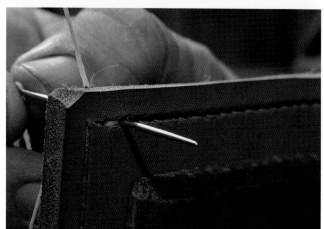

16. Take note that the stitch is placed behind and under the previous one. Be careful to not split the other thread with the needle. If you do split the thread, you must pull the needle back through the hole and make the stitch again. You will not be able to go to the next stitch until this is corrected.

17. Pull the stitch tight with equal tension on both sides. Always go through in the same order on each and every stitch: front to back, then back to front. If you don't, the stitches will be uneven and inconsistent.

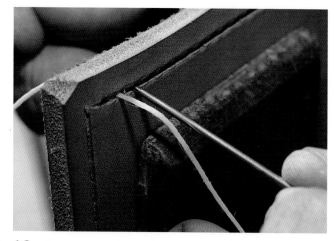

18. Continue stitching by inserting the needle on the front side in the next hole.

19. Pull the thread through until it is tight.

20. Then insert the needle from the back side into the second stitching hole, just as you did for the first stitch, being careful not to split the thread of the front side stitch.

21. Pull this thread through until it is taut. Pull the stitch tight with equal tension on both sides.

22. Continue stitching in the same manner to your last punched hole.

23. When you reach your last punched hole, readjust your project on the pony. Punch more holes until you reach the width of the pony's grip or the end of the leather, whichever comes first. (In this case, it is roughly the same.)

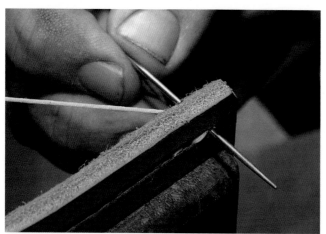

24. Stitch to your last hole. Note that if you were stitching all the way around a project, your last stitch would share the same hole as the first stitch you made.

25. Pull the stitches taut.

26. To secure the stitching when finishing off, you now will backtrack and make another stitch in the previous hole. You will still be following the same sequence of stitching—front to back and then back to front.

27. Because there is already a stitch in this hole, it is a bit tricky to ensure that you do not split any thread with your needle.

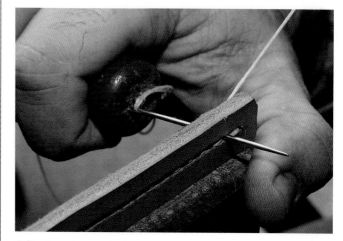

28. Use the end of the stitching awl handle to help push the needle through the hole.

29. Pull the stitches taut.

30. Backtrack one hole again by inserting your needle from front to back in the second hole from the end.

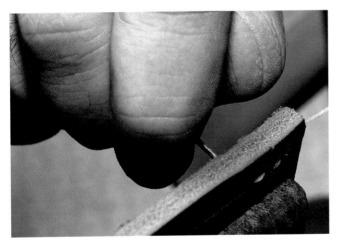

31. Insert the other needle from back to front, being careful to not split the other thread.

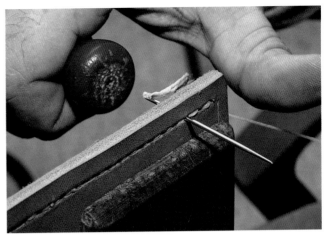

32. Use the end of the stitching awl hilt if needed to push the needle through the hole.

33. Pull the stitches taut.

34. Cut the thread by placing a craft knife blade flat against the leather and pulling the thread back and forth over the blade. This works better than sliding the knife blade back and forth over the thread.

35. Using this method of cutting the thread produces a clean cut that's close to the stitching.

36. Cut the thread on the other side using the same method.

37. The final step is to set the stitches. You will use the overstitch wheel to compress the finished stitches down into the groove. This not only makes the stitching line look better, it helps the stitches last longer because they rest below the surface of the leather.

38. Wet the entire grain side of the leather with clean water and a clean sponge.

39. Place one of the points of the overstitch wheel into the first hole and, with moderate pressure, push the stitches down evenly into the groove.

40. Repeat the process on the other side.

Splicing Stitching Thread

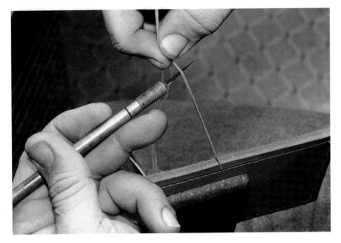

1. Follow these steps when you run out of stitching thread in the middle of a project. Use your craft knife or razor blade to cut both lengths of thread you've been stitching, leaving about 2 inches.

2. Thread two needles onto one length of thread, as before. Insert one needle into the hole two stitches back from where you left off.

3. If necessary, use the end of the stitching awl hilt to push the needle through.

4. Use pliers if necessary to pull the needle through from the flesh side.

5. Pull the thread through until half of the thread is on either side.

6. Insert your needle in the next hole from the grain side to the flesh side and pull the thread through.

7. Place the other needle in the same hole from flesh side to grain side and pull the thread through.

8. Pull both threads until they are drawn tight against the leather.

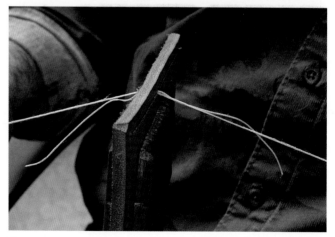

9. Continue stitching in the same manner, this time going into the hole that contains the tails from the previous thread. Pull both threads tight against the leather.

10. Make several more stitches beyond the hole that contains the tails from the previous thread.

11. Use your craft knife to cut the tail close to the stitching.

12. Cut the tail from the grain side in the same manner. Continue stitching using your rethreaded needles.

Raw leather edges that will remain exposed in the final project should be finished for a high-quality appearance. You can start anywhere to bevel, on either the flesh side or the grain side. And beveling can be done on moist or dry leather.

1. Hold the beveler at a 30-degree angle throughout the process.

2. Push the tool away from you using long strokes and a medium amount of downward pressure.

3. Don't be concerned if the leather comes off in short lengths. With practice, you will be able to take off the leather edge in long strips.

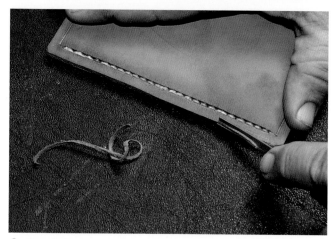

4. Bevel the grain side of the project in the same manner, using long strokes and holding the tool at a 30-degree angle.

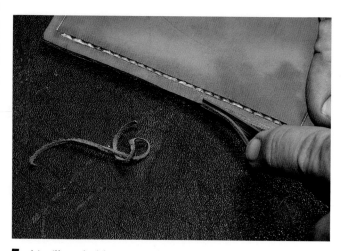

5. You'll probably notice that the grain side is easier to bevel.

6. The rough texture of the bevel will be eliminated when the edge is finished.

Edge Dressing

A nicely finished project edge is the mark of a good craftsperson. The process is easy but does require some elbow grease.

1. Use a wool dauber or good-quality cotton swab to apply a liberal amount of Edge Kote along the entire edge of your project (black is used here).

2. Be extremely careful not to get the dye on the finished side of your project. Should this happen, wipe it off immediately.

3. Let the Edge Kote dry for at least two hours. Then use a small chunk of edge wax to rub an even coat along the entire edge. For belts, this will help the belt go through the loops and add a professional appearance to your project. Straight beeswax could also be used.

4. Use the flat side of a bone tool or Craftool 3-in-1 tool to burnish the top and bottom edges of the bevel to make them smooth and round.

5. Use lots of pressure to compress the fibers of the leather. Wipe off the tool as needed.

6. Rub a wad of ballistic nylon rapidly over the edge in 2- to 3-inch sections. The purpose of this step is to melt the wax and even out the finish. You should feel the leather heat up and see and feel the edge become smooth. Finish by applying Edge Kote over the wax.

7. Applying gum tragacanth to the flesh side will add years to the life of your project. Moisture is leather's biggest enemy, and this finish will add a protective barrier, which is especially important for items used outdoors and for belts, which are exposed to perspiration. Note that gum tragacanth should only be used after the piece is dyed, because it acts like a mask and will prevent any further dyeing or staining.

9. Use the back side of the Craftool 3-in-1 tool or a bone folder to push the liquid into the pores of the leather. Do so by moving the tool in a circular motion while using firm, even pressure. Keep burnishing until the liquid is absorbed and the flesh side has a smooth, shiny finish.

8. Soak a wool dauber with a generous amount of gum tragacanth and apply to the flesh side evenly.

10. The flesh side of this belt is now waterproof and will resist moisture.

Lacing Leather

Before you lace your first project, you may want to practice on a small square first. How much lacing you'll need depends on several things: how tight you pull your stitches, what kind of lace you are using, and how thick your project is. You'll need to lace a few projects and see how much you need of a particular lace to complete a project. It's best to use a length of lacing you can manage so it won't get twisted as you stitch. Procedures to add additional lace are provided on pages 102 and 104.

Procedures to add additional lace are provided on pages 102 and 104.

1. Always work from the front of your project. This test square includes round and square corners, which are laced differently. (The square shown here is composed of two leather pieces cemented together and edge dressed.)

2. The leather should be edge dressed prior to lacing.

3. Start by setting your wing dividers to ¹/₄-inch spacing.

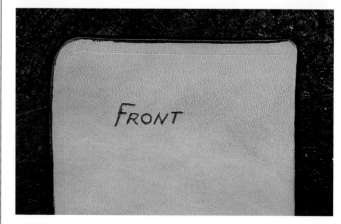

4. Run the wing dividers around the round edge of the dry leather to make a faint line. Follow the curve as you round the corner.

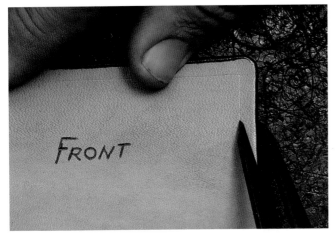

5. When you come to the square corner, follow the edge to make a 90-degree scribe line.

6. All punching should be done on your rubber mat or Poundo board. Begin in the square corner. With your single slot punch, make an impression by pushing the tool into the leather with the edges of the punch meeting the left and right guidelines at a 45-degree angle.

7. Use a single-tong slot punch as a spacer. Place a multiprong punch so it touches that tool and make an impression in the leather along the scribe line.

8. Place the end tongs of the multiprong tool in the last two impressions to line it up then make another set of impressions along the scribe line.

9. When you near the corner, you might have to center the last couple of impressions by eye. Make an angle impression as before in the corner using your single-prong tool. Continue making impressions along the entire perimeter of the piece.

10. Before punching, wipe both sides of the multiprong tool on a piece of ordinary bar soap to lubricate the tongs so they will penetrate the leather cleanly and smoothly.

11. Place the punch on the impressions on the straight line impressions. (The corner slots will be made last.) Strike the punch hard a couple of times with a mallet.

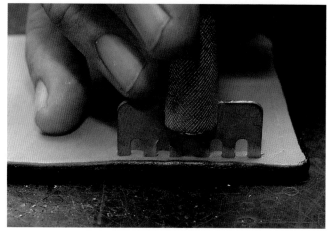

12. The punch should go all the way through the leather.

13. Reset the punch so the first two prongs are placed in the last two existing holes to line up the punch.

14. Be sure to align the tool on the scribe lines. Punch again.

15. If the tool starts to stick, resoap the tines.

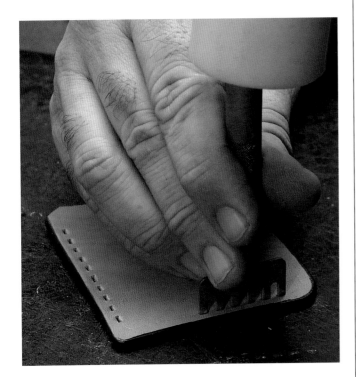

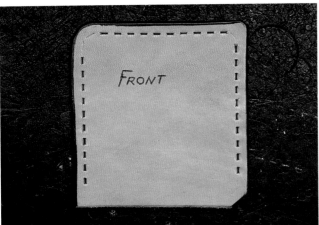

16. Punch all slots on all sides, except for the corner slots. As you approach the rounded corner, don't punch the next-to-last hole, either. This will allow you to adjust the last slot if need be to maintain even spacing.

17. Space the two slots for the round corner by eye so they appear to be evenly spaced, making a light impression in the leather. Punch holes only after you are happy with the spacing.

18. Once all of the straight-edge slots are cut, make the corner cut, with the edges of the tool touching each of the scribe lines at a 45-degree angle.

The Lacing Process

1. Measure out about 3 feet of lacing and cut with a razor blade or scissors.

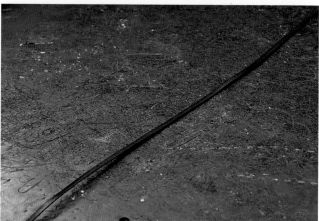

2. Straighten the lace by placing your finger on it with the grain down. Pull the end through and down over a table or rubber mat edge.

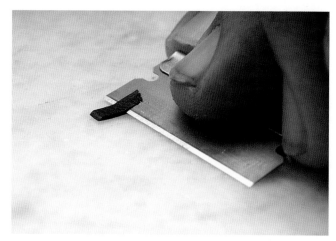

3. Prepare the lace tip by skiving the flesh side edge with a razor blade about $1/2$ inch from the end.

94

4. Your goal is to skive the tip to a feather edge.

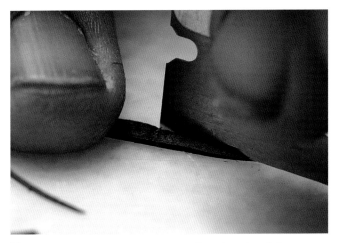

5. Use your razor blade to nick off each side of the tip to create a V shape.

6. This is how your lace end should look.

7. Hold the needle with the prongs facing upward.

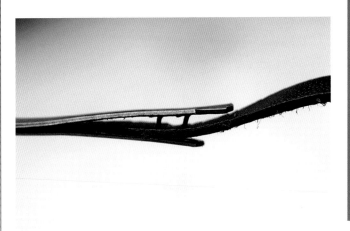

8. With the grain of the lace facing upward, insert the V-shaped end into the needle as far as it will go.

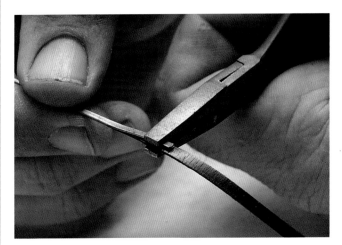

9. Use pliers to gently squeeze the needle closed over the lace.

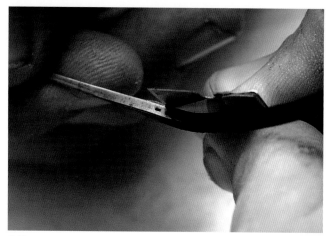

10. Use a razor blade to slice off any lace that protrudes from the edges of the needle.

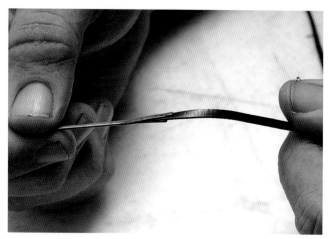

11. You're now ready to begin lacing.

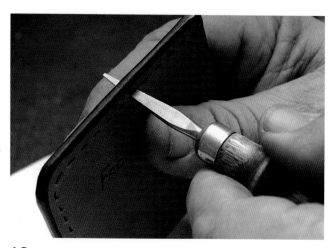

12. Push the lacing awl through each hole only until it opens up. Be sure to keep the awl blade oriented the same way and always push from the front to the back.

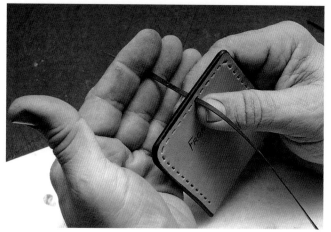

13. With the grain side of the lace facing down, go through the first hole.

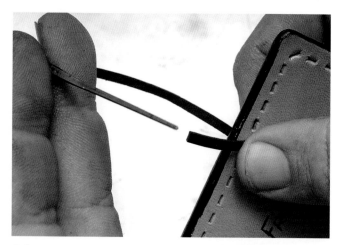

14. Pull the lace through, leaving a 2-inch tail.

15. Keep the lace to the right of the tail.

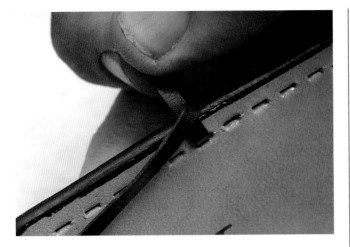

18. Pull the stitch tight.

16. Hold the tail and wrap the lace around it clockwise.

19. This is how your lacing should look.

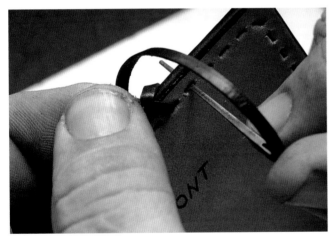

17. While still holding the tail firmly, insert the needle in the next hole to the right, exactly as before.

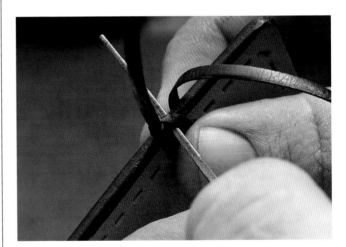

20. Insert the needle underneath the stitch you just made.

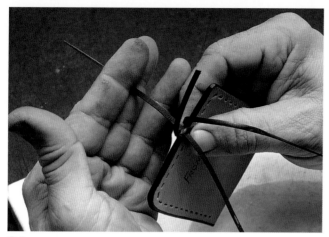

21. Pull the lace through.

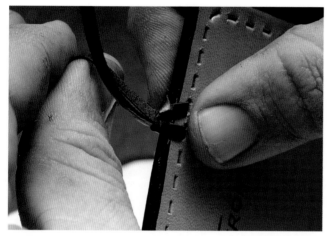

22. Gently tighten the lace.

23. Insert the needle into the third hole and pull through.

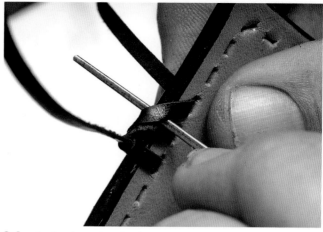

24. Go back under the last stitch you just made, as you did in step 20.

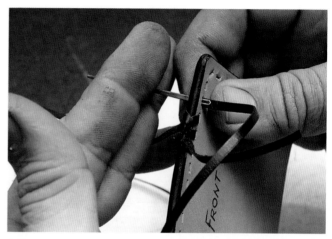

25. Insert the needle into the fourth hole and pull the lace through until it is taut.

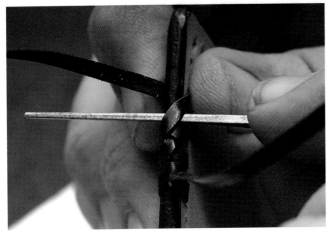

26. Again, place the needle underneath this stitch and pull the lace through until it is taut.

27. If you get the hang of this stitching sequence, you can speed up the process by placing the needle underneath the lace before pulling it taut. This photo and the previous one show the same spot in the process. Notice that the needle is going through the stitch in the same place.

LACING A SQUARE CORNER

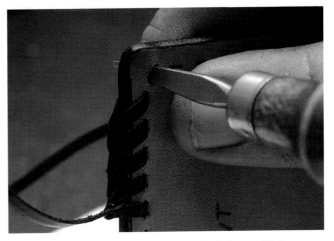

1. Use the awl to make the corner hole larger. To lace a square corner, you will use the exact same stitch, except you will be going through the same hole three times.

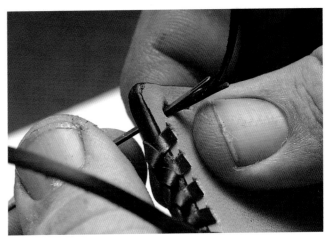

2. Place the needle in the angled corner slot and pull taut.

3. Place the needle underneath the loop you just made and pull through until taut.

4. Place the needle through the same corner hole a second time.

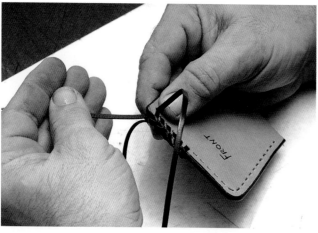

5. Pull the lace through and pull until it is taut inserting the needle underneath the stitch as before.

6. This is how your lacing should look.

7. Use the awl to make the corner hole larger.

8. Place your needle through the same corner hole a third time and make another stitch just as you did in step 5.

9. Use your awl to make the next few holes larger, if necessary.

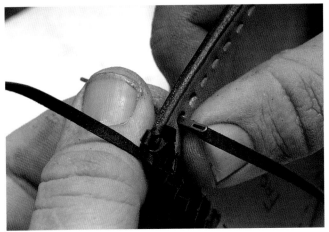

10. Now you can move on by placing your needle in the next straight slot. Make the stitch as before, inserting the needle underneath the stitch you just made.

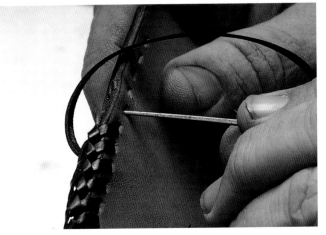

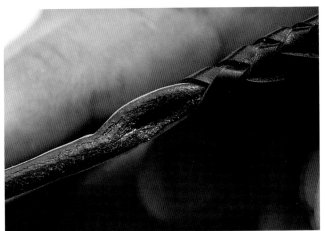

11. Continue stitching, using your awl to make the holes larger as necessary.

13. When you want to add more lace, use your awl to separate the two layers of leather.

12. This is how your lacing should look.

14. Insert your needle through the hole, but go only through the front layer of leather, coming up between the layers.

15. Pull the lace taut.

16. With your razor, cut all but ¼ inch off the remaining lace. Feather the tip to reduce the thickness of the tail.

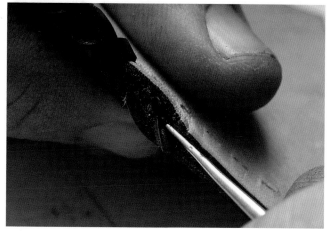

17. Push this ¼-inch end between the two layers using your awl.

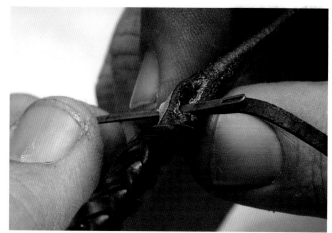

18. Insert the new threaded needle between the layers from front to back.

19. Push the tail of this end between the layers with your awl.

20. Continue the sequence of stitching with the second threaded needle by placing your needle underneath the last stitch you made (from the first threaded needle).

21. Insert your needle in the next hole from front to back. Be sure the two tails are below the needle. Pull the lace taut.

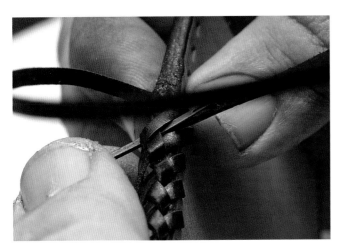

22. Continue by placing the needle underneath the last stitch you made.

Adding Lace to an Unlined Project

If you need additional lace but you don't have two layers to hide the tails, you need to make a "wet splice."

1. Use a razor blade to skive the end off the flesh side of the lace that is attached to the project. Skive to produce a feather edge.

2. Cut the top straight.

3. Skive to a feather edge the end of the grain side of the lace you are attaching.

4. You should have two skived ends: one on the flesh side and one on the grain side.

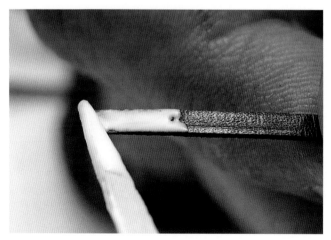

5. Place Leather Weld on one end as shown, completely covering the skived area.

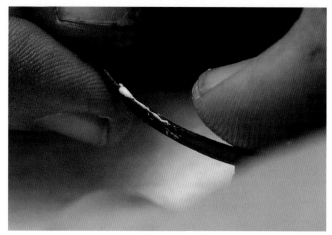

6. Line up the two ends—grain side to flesh side—and press together.

7. Hold the splice for several minutes to allow the glue to set. Let dry about 20 minutes before proceeding.

LACING ROUNDED CORNERS

1. To lace a rounded corner, you go through the corner hole multiple times, just like with a square corner—but this time you will make only two stitches in the hole. Use your awl to open up the corner hole.

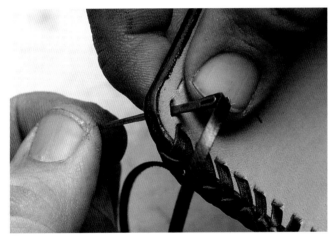

2. Place your needle through the corner hole and draw the lace through until it is taut.

3. Insert your needle underneath the stitch you just made and pull taut.

4. Place your needle through the corner hole again and pull through until the lace is taut.

5. Again, place your needle underneath the previous stitch and pull until taut.

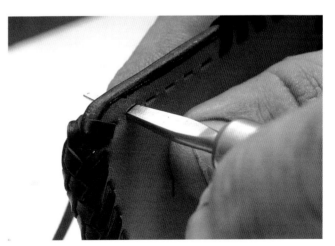

6. Use your awl to open up the hole next to the corner hole and continue with the standard stitch sequence.

Finishing Off

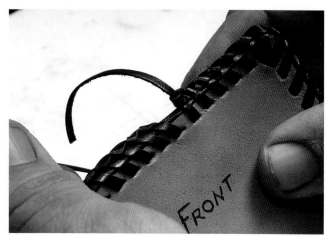

1. Proceed until all holes have been laced.

2. Use your awl to split the leather to make room for the lacing ends.

3. Next, you need to pull the tail from the first lacing stitch you made through the loop without disturbing the loop. To do so, insert the pointed end of your spoon tool into the loop. If this loop untwists, you'll need to pull the lace from the loop of the next stitch and try again.

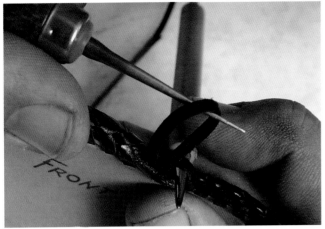

4. Hold the spoon tool that's holding the loop and your project with one hand. With the other, use the awl to pull the tail through the loop and let it hang.

5. Carefully remove the spoon tool from the loop. Insert your needle into this loop from the top.

6. Pull the needle and lace through the loop. Leave a small loop instead of tightening the lace down.

7. Put the needle through the slot left empty by the tail.

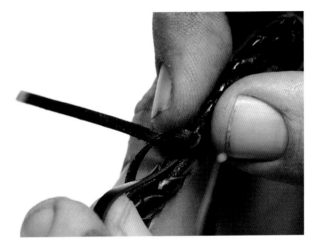

8. Pull the lace that's connected to the needle until the loop closes securely.

9. Note how this loop falls between the tail and the lace connected to the needle.

10. Insert the needle through this loop.

11. Note that the tail and the lace still connected to the needle are next to another. At this point, you want to use your fingers to manipulate the stitches until they lie flat and are evenly spaced. You may need to use your awl to loosen and tighten various stitches until they lie flat.

12. Once you are satisfied with the stitch placement, hold the two strips of lace taut. Place your craft knife or razor blade against the stitches, close to the other stitching, and cut the tails off.

13. This is how the final lacing looks.

108

14. Roll your mallet handle back and forth across the lace to burnish and flatten it. Don't press too hard or you will damage the lace.

CORRECTING TWISTED STITCHES

1. You must always keep your needle oriented with the grain side down to help prevent the lace from twisting. If you notice you have made a twisted stitch, take out all of the stitches after the point where the lace is twisted.

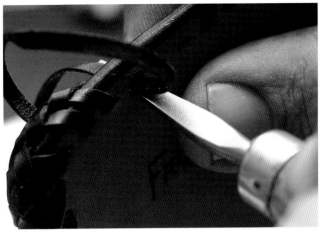

2. To take out stitches, loosen the stitches so there is room to work. Use your awl to enlarge the hole so that the lace may be removed without breaking or stretching it.

3. After enlarging the hole, place your needle through from back to front. When you reach the twisted stitch, take it out, untwist your lace, and continue.

Applying a Finishing Product

Although Leather Balm with Atom Wax will not water-proof your project, it will add a measure of protection and give the leather a nice soft sheen. (If you do want to make your project moisture-resistant, you can use an acrylic coating, such as Super Sheen.)

1. Don't shake Leather Balm prior to applying, to avoid creating unwanted air bubbles. Place a generous amount on a clean, lint-free cloth.

2. Gently apply the wax to the entire grain side of the project, including any areas that are folded under. Don't press too hard.

3. Wait about 15 minutes then buff using a clean side of the applicator cloth.

Cleaning and Conditioning

Before you apply any product to your leather, you should test it on a scrap piece of leather dyed or painted with the same products already on your project. If that's not possible, test on an inconspicuous portion of your project. Some products may pull the dye out, leaving an unsightly mess.

To clean leather: Start by using a soft brush to remove loose dirt then wipe with a soft cloth. If you need more cleaning power, use a mild product that does not strip the natural oils out of the leather. Be wary of multi-function products, such as those that claim to clean and protect. These may leave a greasy film behind that will clog pores and could lead to bacteria formation. Over time, bacteria will eat away at the leather and break down the stitching. A final tip: Never use saddle soap on anything other than a saddle; it will destroy items made from thinner leather.

To condition leather: When a leather item starts showing signs of stiffness, it is time to condition. A good conditioner is usually a lanolin-based product that will replace natural oils and fats. Those that contain petroleum or mineral oils can damage leather over time. Apply the conditioner as directed on the product label.

To treat water spots: Moisture is leather's biggest enemy. If water spots are treated while they are still wet, there's a chance you can disguise them by wetting the entire piece as in the tooling process and placing it away from direct heat to dry.

Mildew is more difficult to correct. The mildew damage shown here is most likely too severe to fix, although it may be possible to mask the problem by coloring the piece with an oil-based black dye.

3

Putting It All Together

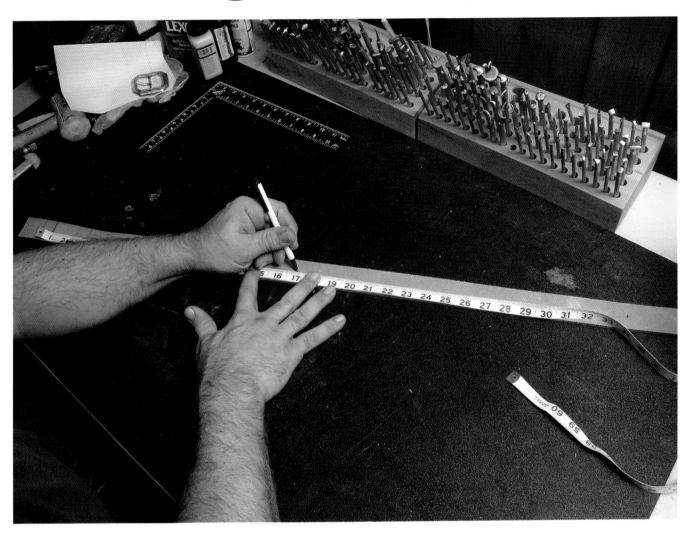

The more you practice various leatherworking techniques, the better your final work will be. Of course, the most enjoyable way to test your skills is to actually make something. In this chapter, we'll put all the basic techniques from the past chapter together to demonstrate the creation of a belt and a card case. A variety of useful accessories can be created using the same basic techniques, and a photo gallery of them is included at the end of the book.

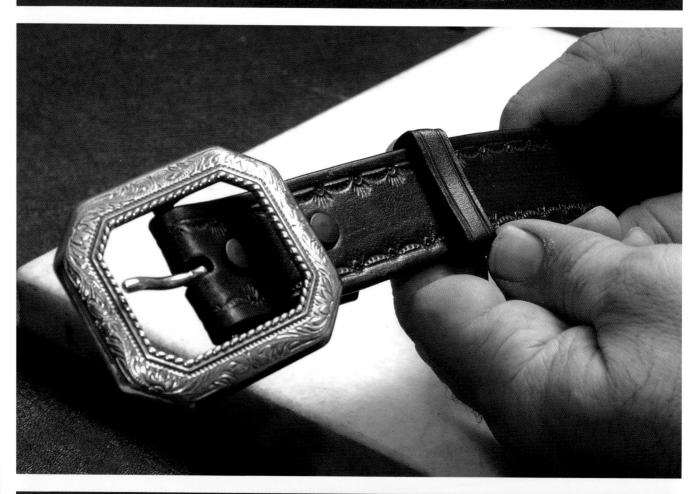

Tools and Supplies

- Smooth marble, polyester, or other hard surface for stamping design.
- Appropriate surface for punching holes and setting fasteners (Poundo board, linoleum square, or 10-ounce cowhide square).
- 8- to 9-ounce vegetable-tanned cowhide leather belt strap, $1^1/_2$ inches wide by waist size plus 8 inches. Refer to information on how to size a belt on the next page).
- $1^1/_2$-inch heel bar buckle
- Three conchos (optional)
- Snaps and snap setter

- 8- to 9-ounce scrap leather for testing stamps
- Scratch awl
- $^1/_4$-inch oblong hole punch
- $^3/_4$-inch or 1-inch oblong bag hole punch
- Skiver
- Size 2 edge beveler
- Leather shears
- Utility knife
- Mallet
- Veiner, seeder, and camouflage stamps or stamps of your choice (Craftool V 406, S 705, and C 834 were used here).

- Leather conditioner
- Gel antique stain
- Edge wax and burnishing fabric
- Edge Kote
- Bone tool
- Gum tragacanth
- Small bowl of clean water and clean cellulose sponge
- Measuring square
- Measuring tape
- Cotton swabs or wool daubers
- Scrap rags
- Ballpoint pen
- Index card

Sizing the Belt

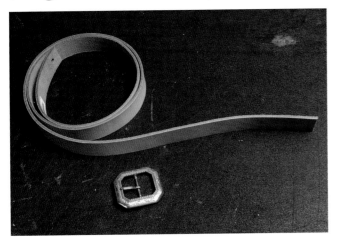

1. Start with a belt strap and center bar buckle.

2. Measure the distance from the bar to the inside edge of the leading edge of the buckle.

3. Make note of this distance (here, it's $^7/_8$ inch).

4. While wearing the type of pants the belt will go with, take a measurement around the waist where the belt will be worn.

Belt Diagram

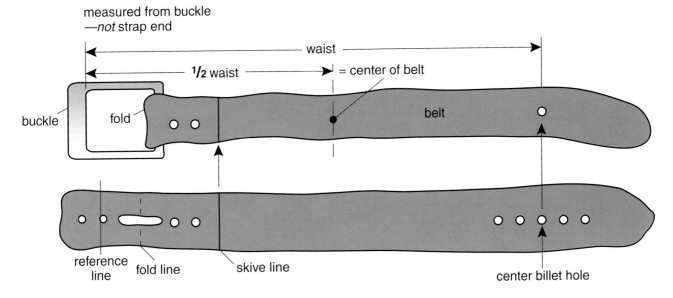

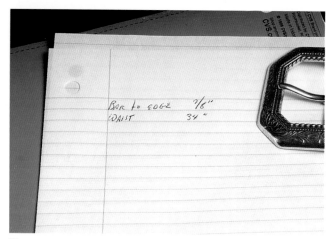

5. Make note of the measurement (in this case, it's 34 inches).

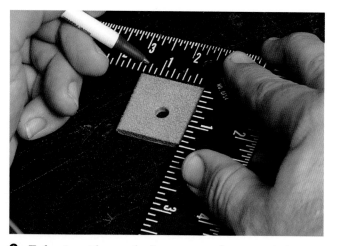

6. To begin with a perfectly square end on your belt strap, use your square to mark a perpendicular line about 1½ inches from the edge. (Here, we are also removing the hole that was used to hang the belt blank in the store.)

7. Use a ballpoint pen on the flesh side to mark the perpendicular line.

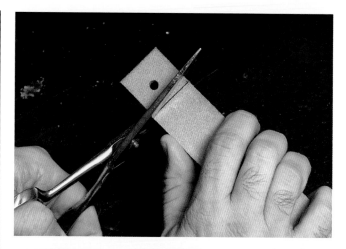

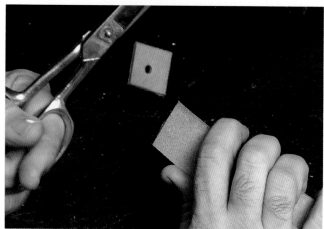

8. Use shears to carefully cut along the line.

9. Measure 5 inches from the squared end and make a mark with the pen on the flesh side of the leather.

114

10. Make a perpendicular line at the mark using your square and pen. This line represents the skive line.

11. From the skive line, make a mark 2¹/₂ inches toward the buckle end.

12. Draw a line at this point. This will be the fold line.

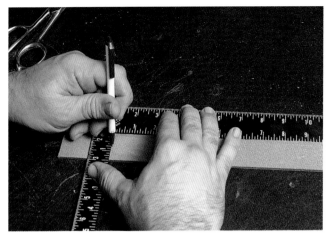

13. While the square is still positioned, mark the center of the line you just made at the center of the strip.

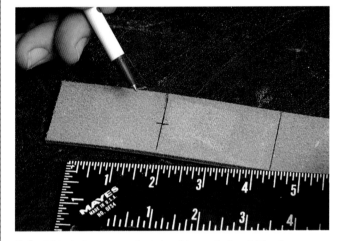

14. This is how your belt buckle end should look now.

15. The next measurement is derived from the buckle measurement your recorded in step 3 (⅞ inch here). Use the measurement of the actual buckle you are using.

16. From the fold line you just made (which is 2¹/₂ inches from the end of the belt strap) measure ⁷/₈ inch (the buckle measurement) toward the end of the leather strap. This line represents where the inside edge of the buckle meets the leather of the finished belt.

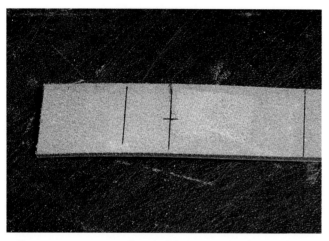

17. As before, draw a line with your ballpoint pen on the flesh side of the belt. It is from this reference line that you will determine all other belt measurements.

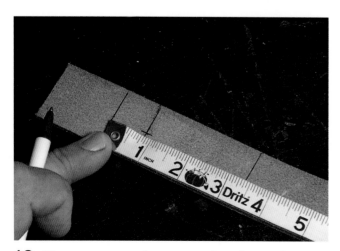

18. Place your measuring tape on the reference line as shown.

19. Measure from the reference line to the other end of the belt using the waist measurement you recorded in step 5 (34 inches here).

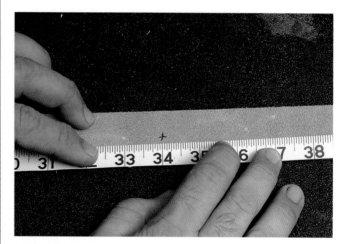

20. Make a plus sign in the center the belt at this point. This represents the center hole of five holes.

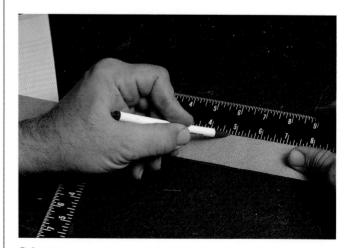

21. From this center hole mark, measure 4³/₄ inches to the billet end of the belt. This mark represents the end of the belt strap.

116

22. As before, use a ballpoint pen to make a perpendicular line at the mark on the flesh side, using the square.

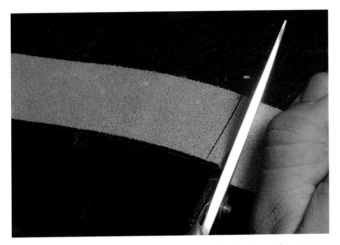

23. Use the leather shears to cut the belt about ¼ inch beyond the billet end.

CONCHO PLACEMENT

At this point, you will want to decide if you will be adding decorative elements, such as conchos, to your belt.

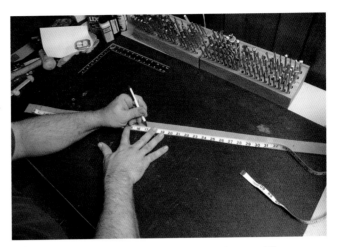

1. If so, mark the center back of the belt now. The center is between the center hole line in the billet end (step 20) and the reference line (step 17).

2. The center point is half the belt waist measurement. In this project, it is half of 34 inches: 17 inches. Make a pen mark that shows where the center concho will be placed.

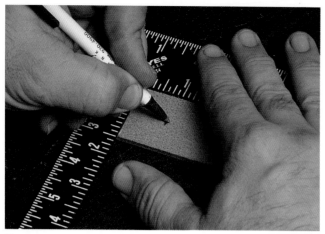

3. Make a plus sign in the center of the strip at this point.

4. The center mark is used to place any belt back decorations and should be transferred to the grain side with your awl for future reference.

5. To keep the hole small and unobtrusive, do not punch your awl with a mallet. Push the awl by hand just far enough to make a small hole that shows through on the grain side.

Cutting the Billet End

1. Transfer the line from the flesh side of the billet end of the belt to the grain side by marking along the edge of the belt. Make a mark on the grain side.

2. Use the square to draw a perpendicular line across the grain side of the belt. Make a mark at the center point along this line.

3. You can use a strap end cutter at this point to neatly cut the end of the belt to shape. Or, if you don't want to purchase a strap end cutter, you can use a simple pattern made by tracing the end of a belt you already have or by drawing one freehand on a strip of paper folded in half. Place your belt tip pattern on the grain side of the belt as shown, with the edges even and the point at the center dot.

4. Using the ballpoint pen, trace the outline of the pattern onto the grain side of the belt.

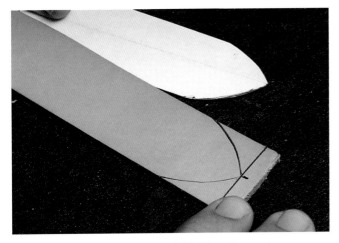

5. This is how your belt should look at this point.

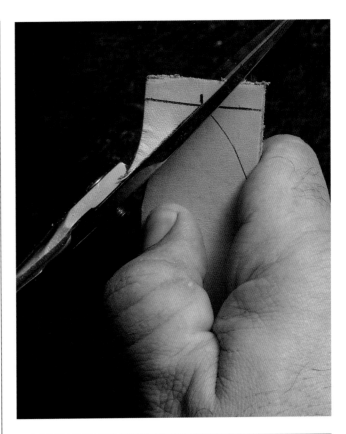

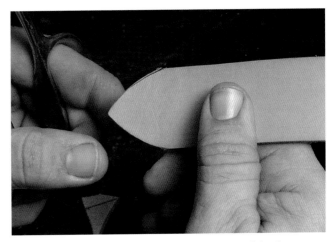

6. With shears, carefully cut on the inside of the lines from each side to the tip of the belt end.

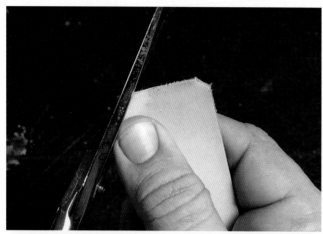

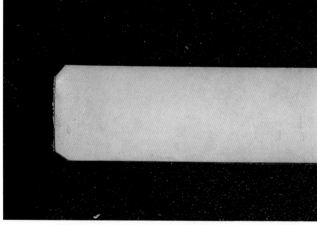

7. Turn your attention to the buckle end of the belt. To create a professional appearance, use shears to snip off a portion of each corner on an angle, as shown.

Preparing the Leather for Stamping

Wet the entire piece—both the flesh and grain sides—each and every time prior to stamping to prevent permanent water spots. Use a light touch. Pressing too hard or scrubbing could abrade the grain and ruin the finish.

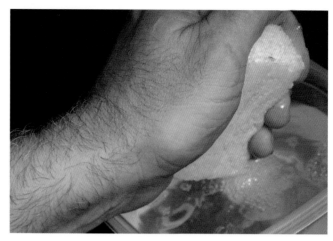

1. Dampen a new palm-sized piece of cellulose sponge and wring it out lightly so water isn't dripping.

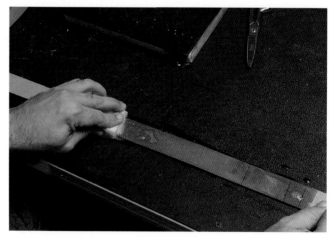

2. Starting from one end of the flesh side of the belt, generously wet the entire length of the leather evenly with the sponge.

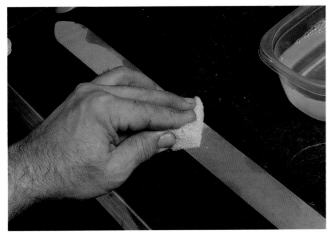

3. Flip the belt over and repeat the process on the grain side, using about half the amount of water you used on the flesh side.

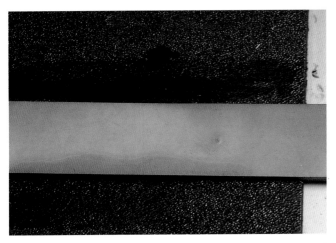

4. Spots that are more porous will typically dry faster and give the piece a spotty appearance. This will disappear as the leather dries.

5. After wetting the leather, you should add a leather conditioner on the grain side right away.

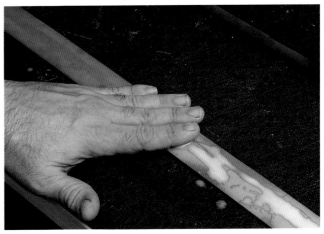

6. Use your fingers to massage the leather in a circular motion until the leather conditioner disappears and your fingers start to drag a bit. This indicates that the conditioner has soaked into the leather.

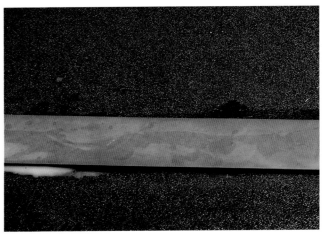

7. Some mottling is normal as the leather dries, due to normal inconsistencies in the hide. Wait until the leather dries to the proper point before stamping.

Making a Stamping Guideline

The next step is to make an impression in the leather to serve as a guideline for stamping. The easiest way for this belt project is to use the Craftool 3-in-1 tool, which has a ¹/₈-inch groove. If you do not have this tool or want to make a wider guideline, you may use dividers for this purpose. This procedure is shown on page 126.

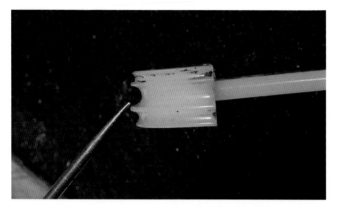

1. The 3-in-1 tool has groovers for burnishing the edges of leather. It is used here to make a guideline.

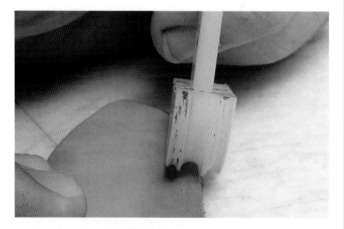

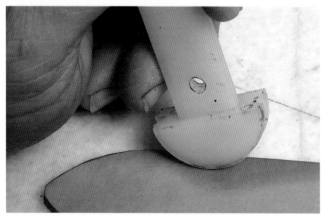

2. Place your belt on the stamping surface. Place the tool against the straight portion of the belt edge as shown. The curved billet ends will be done last. Once the tool is in position, you may find it more comfortable to hold the handle closer to the tool.

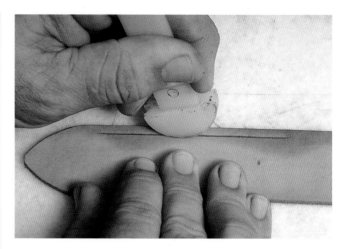

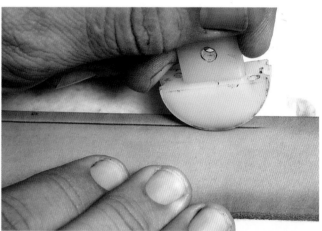

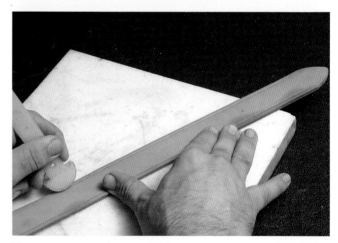

3. Using heavy downward pressure, move the tool forward and backward in about 3-inch segments along the entire length of the belt. As you go, the tool will make a dark line on the leather. You will notice that the tool will drag at first, but as the leather burnishes, it will become slicker. When that happens, the tool will slide more easily.

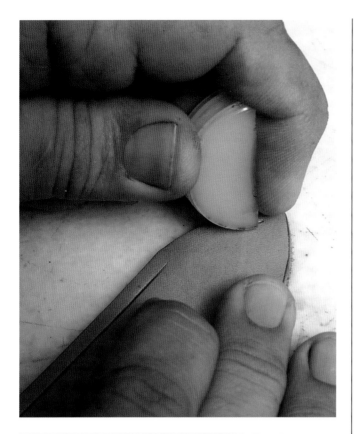

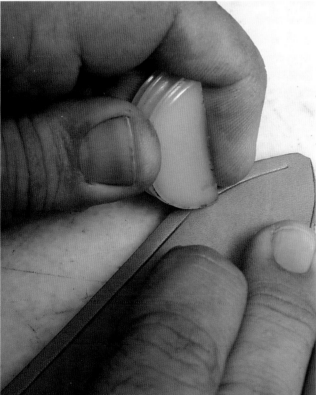

Using wing dividers to make guidelines

An alternate method of making tooling guide lines is to use a wing divider tool. Allow wet leather to dry to the proper wetness. Adjust the dividers to $1/8$ inch or the setting you prefer. Run one arm of the tool along the belt edge, allowing the weight of the other arm to make the line. Don't press or you risk permanently scoring the leather. Other tools you may use to make a guideline include an awl and a stylus.

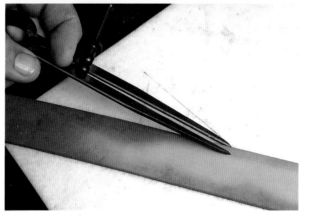

4. Take off the handle and finish the curved billet end by starting at the tip and proceeding to the existing guideline.

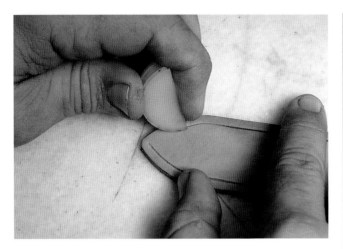

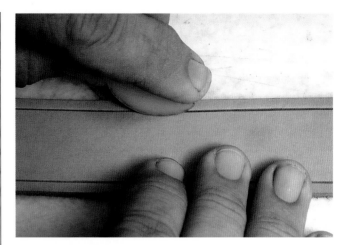

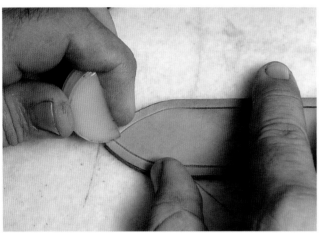

5. Repeat the process on the other side.

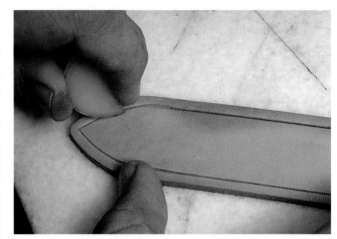

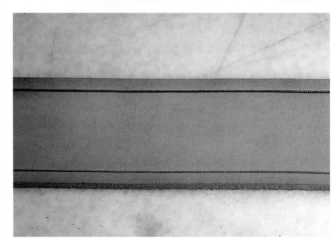

6. Use the head of the 3-in-1 tool to go along the entire edge a second time, pushing down hard. Be sure to stay in the track you made the first time. You'll notice that the groove will become slicker as you go.

Stamping

If you find you don't have the exact veiner, seeder, and camouflage tools shown here, substitute a similar tool.

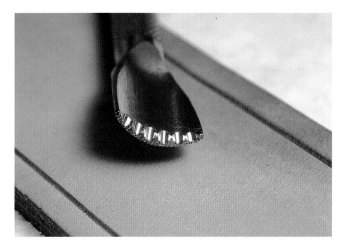

Craftool Veiner V 406

Craftool Seeder S 705

Craftool Camouflage Tool C 834

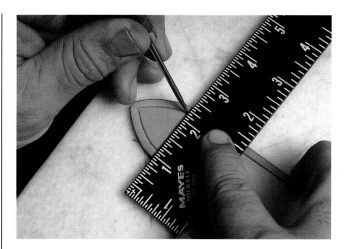

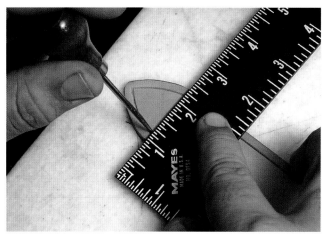

1. Use an awl to make very slight indentations on the guideline where the billet end curve straightens out.

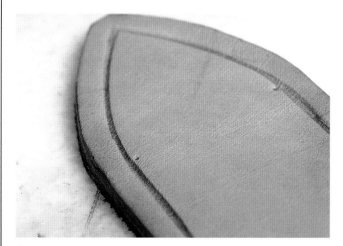

2. These marks are where you will begin making your decorative stamped border.

3. Set your divider tool just slightly larger than the width of the stamp (here, it's the veiner).

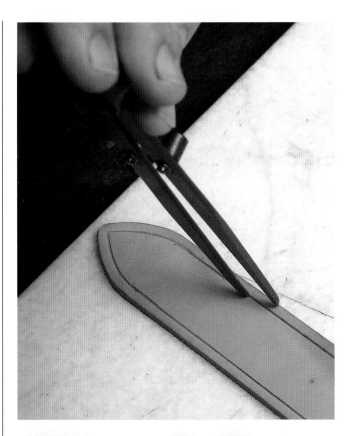

4. Place one arm of the divider on the awl mark and the other just inside the divider line toward the center of the belt. Press the tool on the leather lightly, using just enough pressure to make a light mark.

5. Place the one divider arm in the second mark you just made and "walk" the divider down the belt to make evenly spaced marks. Take your time with this process to ensure that you will have reliable marks to stamp your design. These marks will disappear as the belt is tooled.

6. Center the veiner tool between the two marks. The tool should be on the line, but toward the center. With the tool perpendicular to the work surface, tap the tool firmly two or three times. As a rule, the larger the stamping tool, the harder you need to strike it with the mallet.

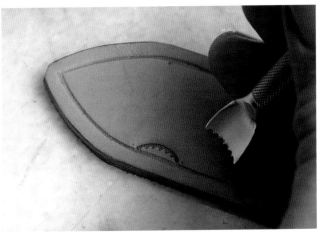

7. The tool impression should result in nice dark lines. If the leather is "mushing" out, you are pounding too hard or the leather is too wet. Try to stamp all impressions at the same depth.

8. Continue stamping between the marks for about 4 or 5 inches. Leave enough space between impressions for the seeder stamp, which you will add later.

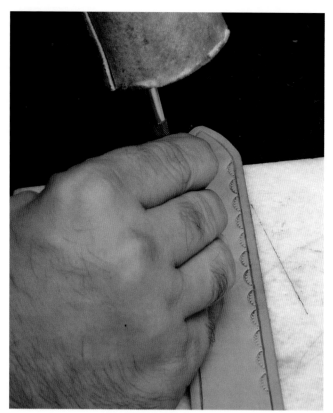

10. Continue stamping, rotating the belt every 4 or 5 inches as you go.

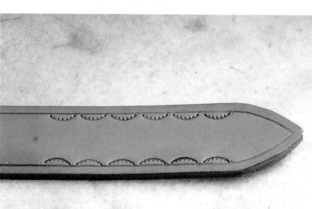

9. To prevent the belt from deforming or stretching out of shape, turn it around and start stamping the opposite edge. Stop stamping at the same point on each side.

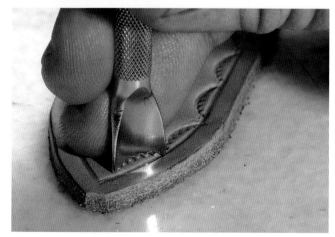

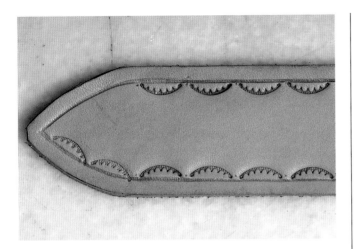

11. The TLAR ("that looks about right") method is used for spacing the veiner stamp at the tip of the belt. Estimate the spacing and stamp the final two impressions on each side.

12. Now place the seeder tool just above and inside the guideline between the veiner stamps. With the tool perpendicular to the work surface, use the mallet to strike the tool once. Use a light touch. If you hit the seeder tool too hard, it may go right through the belt.

13. It is not necessary to periodically switch sides with the seeder tool, as it covers less area than the veiner tool and won't deform the leather belt shape.

14. Place the camouflage tool so that the half-moon shape surrounds the seeder impression.

15. With the tool in a perpendicular position, strike the mallet one or two times.

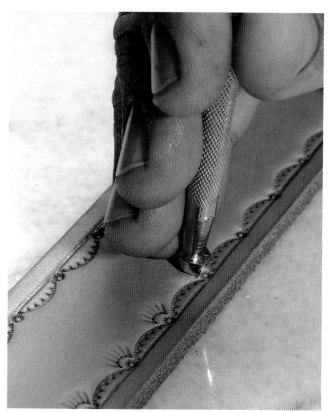

16. Continue to make an impression over each seeder mark except for the one at the very tip of the billet end. Be sure to set your stamp at the same angle for each impression.

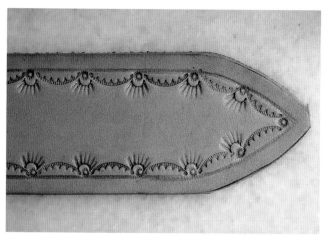

17. The finished design. Experiment on scrap leather with different tools to create your own one-of-a-kind belt design.

Beveling the Edges

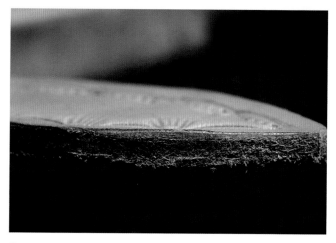

1. Raw leather edges are unsightly and should be finished for a professional-looking job.

2. A size 2 edge beveler was used for this project.

3. Keep the tool at a 30-degree angle during the entire process. Push the tool away from you using long strokes and a medium amount of pressure.

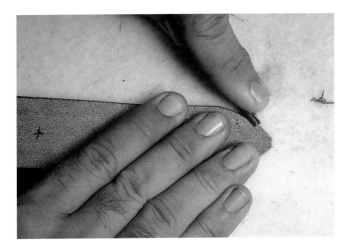

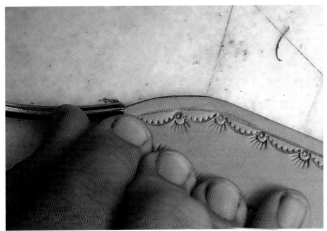

4. Go slowly and use shorter strokes when beveling the billet end. Bevel the grain and the flesh side of the entire belt.

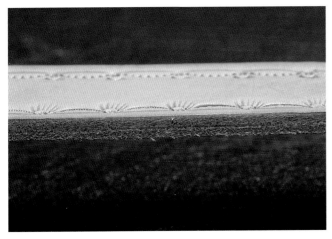

5. The belt edge after beveling is smooth and has a well-crafted appearance.

Punching Billet-End Holes

1. Place the belt flesh side up on a rubber mat or Poundo board. You will now make a centered line that extends about 4 inches from either side of the plus sign, which represents your center hole mark. Use a pencil—*not* a pen—to make several light marks in the center of the belt (³/₄ inch on this 1¹/₂-inch-wide belt.)

Note: A pen was used here to make the marks and line easy to see. The pencil marks and line will remain after the belt is finished. If you prefer not to have any marks on the finished belt, use wing dividers to make slight indentations.

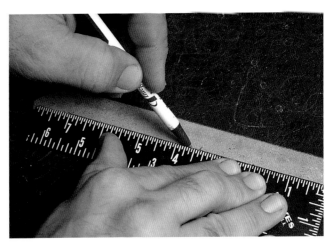

2. Use a pencil to lightly draw the center line, which will be your guideline for punching your belt holes.

3. This is how your line should look.

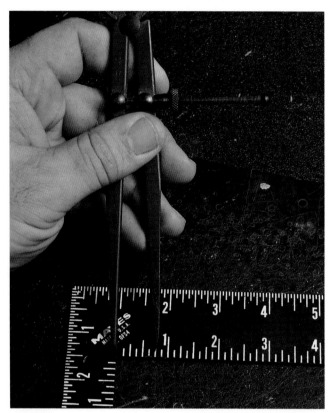

4. Billet end holes are generally placed ³/4 inch apart in standard belts. Set the wing divider at ³/4 inch.

5. Place one arm of the divider on the plus sign and make a mark on either side of this point.

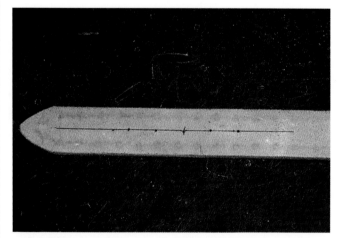

6. Place one arm on one of the marks you just made and make a mark on the far side of this point. Repeat the process using the other mark from step 6 to make the last mark. You should now have five marks that are ³/4 inch apart, two on either side of the plus sign.

7. Use an awl and mallet to make holes all the way through the leather on all five marks.

8. Flip your belt so that the grain side is facing upward. Here you may either use a $1/4$-inch round hole punch or a $1/4$-inch oblong hole punch. Oblong holes protect the leather from stretching a bit better than round holes.

9. Set your punch over each hole and carefully press the tool lightly into the leather at a 90-degree angle just to make a light impression.

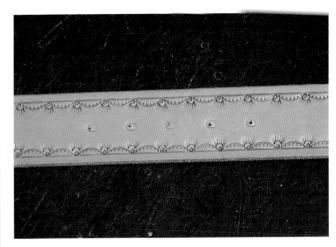

10. If you are not satisfied with the placement, go back and reset the tool and make another light impression.

11. When you are satisfied with your punch placement marks, reregister the tool over the final mark. Hold the punch at a 90-degree angle to the belt. Strike the mallet hard as many times as necessary to go through the leather.

12. Note that all punch holes are done from the grain side of the leather. Continue punching until all five marks are punched through.

Skiving and Beveling the Buckle End

1. Skiving is done after tooling. But before skiving, let your belt thoroughly dry for at least 24 hours

2. The purpose of skiving the buckle end is to reduce the thickness of the leather at the fold line area. This will make your fold lay flat and make room for the buckle between the two layers of leather.

3. Skive from the skive line to the end of the belt. The goal is to remove about a third of the thickness of the leather.

4. Take your time with this step. Remove thin shavings in short, even strokes. Remember to keep turning the skiver in different directions as you proceed.

5. Skive to the end of the belt. Don't make deep cuts that will take off a lot of material at a time; work in short, thin strokes.

6. Skive the center, sides, and end of this area. Strive for a consistent thickness of leather over the entire skived area.

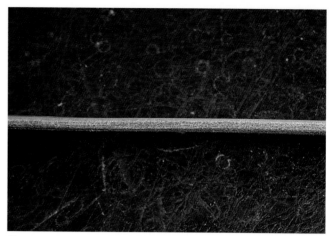

8. The belt buckle end before skiving.

7. Use the edge beveler to rebevel all the edges that were skived.

9. There is a noticeable difference in thickness after the belt buckle end has been skived. The finished thickness should be about two thirds of the original thickness. You do not want to remove more than half the thickness, as this would make the belt less durable.

Punching the Oblong Tongue Hole

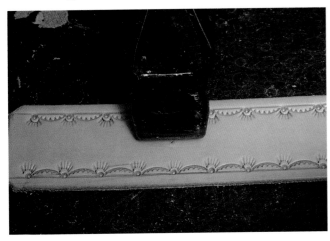

1. The awl hole you made at the buckle end early in the process represents the center of the tongue hole. The tongue is the metal rod that goes through the billet-end holes to hold the belt in the buckle. You may use a ³/₄-inch or 1-inch oblong bag punch.

2. This punch is made from the grain side. Center the punch over the small awl hole by eye.

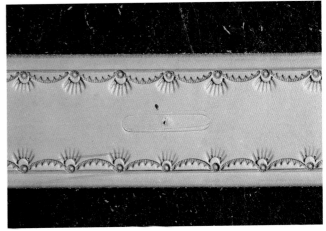

3. Place the punch at a 90-degree angle and push down with both hands to make an impression in the leather. Check the impression and relocate if necessary.

Note: An alternate method using a ¼-inch round hole punch will also be shown.

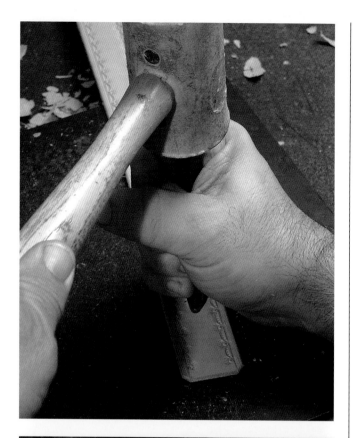

4. Once you're satisfied with the placement, register the punch. Remember to make your punch on a rubber mat or Poundo board so as not to damage your tool or work surface. Hold the punch at a 90-degree angle and rap solidly with the mallet several times until the punch goes all the way through the leather.

AN ALTERNATE METHOD: USING A ¼-INCH ROUND HOLE PUNCH

1. Find the awl hole you made earlier.

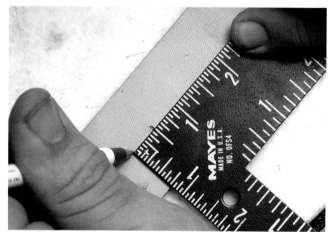

2. Make a mark ½ inch to the left of the center mark.

3. Make a mark ½ to the right of the center mark.

4. Prepare a 1/4-inch round hole punch by rubbing the edges and inside with soap.

5. Make light registration marks with your hole punch to ensure that your placement is correct. Then punch both holes by tapping several times with your mallet using firm pressure.

6. Line up your straight edge along the outer edges of both holes.

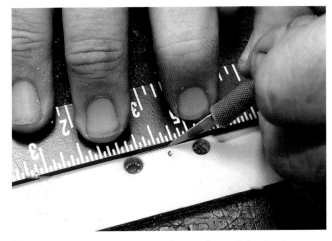

7. Use a craft knife to score the surface of the leather from the center of the first hole to the center of the second hole.

8. Repeat the process between the two holes on the other side.

9. Be careful not to score beyond the center of the hole, as was done here. (This small goof will be removed in the beveling process.)

10. Use your craft knife to cut all the way through the leather on both scored lines.

11. Press out the oblong leather piece with your craft knife.

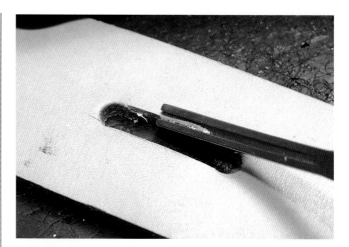

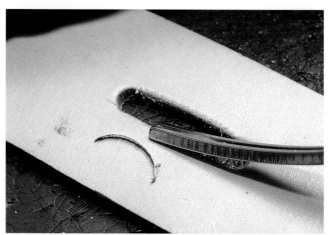

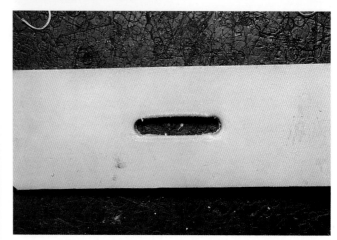

12. Use your edge beveler to dress up the edges of the oblong hole.

Coloring, Finishing, and Folding the Belt

Choosing a color finish is an art in itself and a matter of personal preference. For this project, Eco-Flo Gel Antique Mahogany was used. This product is also available in black, tan, saddle tan, and medium and dark brown. Don't forget to dye your belt keeper the same time you dye your belt.

1. Start by squirting a moderate amount of gel onto a medium wool dauber. Apply the gel generously to the entire grain side, making sure the dye penetrates the recesses of the stamp impressions.

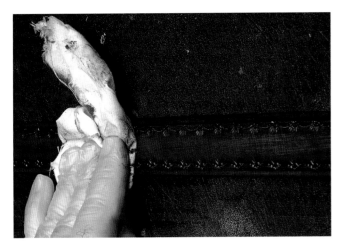

2. Use a clean, lint-free rag or old t-shirt to rub the gel into the leather and wipe off excess. Apply more gel if needed in recesses that may have been missed. Apply more gel to the dauber and repeat the process on the flesh side of the belt. Check the belt edges to make sure they are dyed, as well.

Rub the gel into the leather and wipe off excess gel. When you are satisfied, let the belt dry for 24 hours.

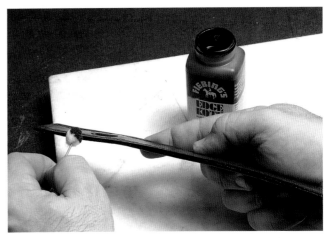

3. Use a wool dauber or good-quality cotton swab to apply a liberal amount of Edge Kote along the entire edge of your belt. Be extremely careful to not get the dye on the top finished side of the belt or other project. Should this happen, wipe it off immediately. Let the Edge Kote dry for about 2 hours before proceeding. Once it is dry, use a small chunk of the edge wax to rub an even coat along the entire edge.

4. Burnish the edge by rubbing a wad of ballistic or sports nylon swiftly over the edge in 2- to 3-inch sections.

5. Use the flat side of a bone tool or the Craftool 3-in-1 tool to burnish the edges to make them round and smooth.

Next, use a wool dauber to apply a generous amount of gum tragacanth to the flesh side. Use the flat side of the Craftool 3-in-1 tool or bone folder to burnish in a circular motion. Keep burnishing until the liquid is pushed into the pores of the leather and the flesh side has a smooth, shiny finish. The flesh side of this belt will now resist moisture. Let the belt dry overnight before proceeding.

6. Although this step runs counter to previous warnings about leather and water, it's a must. You cannot fold dry leather without cracking it. So you must wet the entire belt (to prevent water stains) so the buckle end can be folded to hold the buckle. Run the belt under hot water for about three to four minutes to give the fibers a chance to absorb the moisture. The leather must be wet all the way through at the point of the fold.

7. Fold the grain side of the belt end to the back in the center of the oblong hole

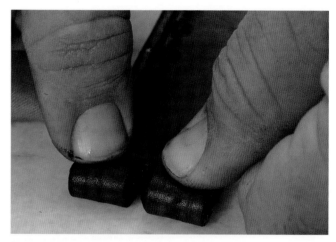

8. Squeeze both sides firmly together. Place waxed paper over the belt to protect it and weigh it down with any flat, heavy object, such as the stone slab, and let it dry overnight.

9. The belt end is now ready for the snaps and buckle.

Adding Conchos

1. Find the awl hole you made in the center back of the belt. Use your awl to make the hole visible on the other side.

2. Use your wing dividers to determine the placement of the concho to the right of the center. There's no rule for spacing conchos—place them where they look best to you. Use the awl to mark the placement, in the center of the width of the belt.

3. With the wing dividers set to the same spacing, mark the spot for the left concho. Again, use your ruler to determine the center width point.

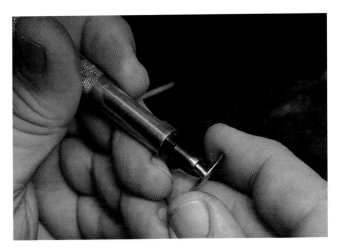

4. Select a round hole punch that is the right size for your concho shaft.

143

5. Place the hole punch over each mark and make a light impression by pushing the punch down. Check your impressions to be sure the placement is correct.

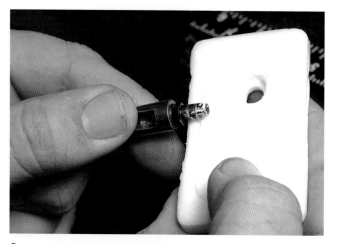

6. Coat the outside of the tool with ordinary bar soap to help the punch go through the leather smoothly.

7. Remember to punch only on your rubber mat or Poundo board. Place the punch on the grain side at a 90-degree angle and hit it hard with the mallet until the punch goes all the way through the leather. Punch the remaining two holes in the same manner, soaping the punch each time.

8. Switch to your stone slab or other hard surface. You'll need a concave anvil for the next step. The anvil's shape will protect the concho from becoming disfigured.

9. Place the decorative side of the concho down onto the anvil. Line up the center hole of the belt with the concho so that the concho shaft pops through the grain side of the belt.

144

10. Place the concho back onto the shaft.

11. Use the snap and rivet setter to tap the back onto the front the concho.

12. Place the tool over the concho back at a 90-degree angle.

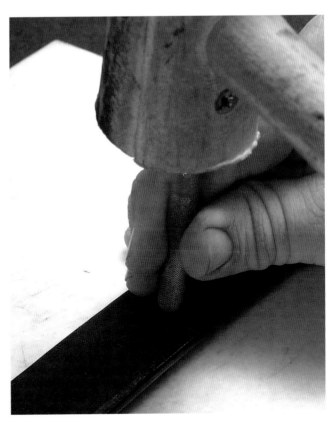

13. Tap gently but firmly in a circular motion to set the entire circumference of the concho. Be careful not to hit the tool too hard, so you don't smash the metal.

14. Here's how the front and back of your concho should look. Repeat the process to attach the other two conchos.

15. Check to see if the conchos are attached properly by trying to slide your fingernail under the edge. If it goes under, the concho is too loose and should be tapped some more.

16. These silver metal conchos contrast nicely with the dark belt color. Once you locate the center of the belt, you can use your wing dividers to place multiple decorative elements wherever it pleases you.

Making Snap or Rivet Holes

1. Measure $7/8$ inch from the fold line of the belt to place the first snap or rivet hole.

2. Find the center of the width.

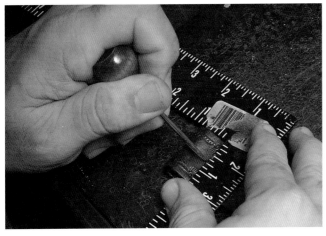

3. Make a mark at this point with your awl.

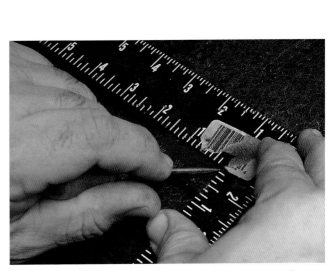

4. Measure $1^1/4$ inches from that mark to position the second snap hole.

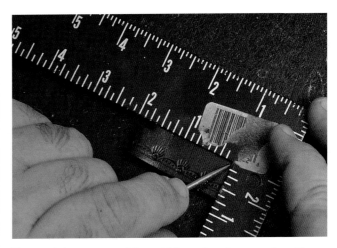

5. Find the center of the width and make a mark with your awl

6. Center a $1/4$-inch hole punch over your marks and push down to make a light impression.

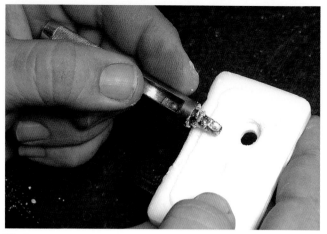

7. Use soap to coat the tool to make it easier to punch.

9. The belt is ready for the addition of snaps or rivets.

Snaps were used for this project to allow the buckle to be easily switched. Rivets are permanent fasteners—once they are installed, the buckle can't be changed.

If you are using snaps, add them now. If you are using rivets you'll need to add them as you put the buckle and keeper on.

8. Before punching, check that the strap sides are even and parallel. With the tool at a 90-degree angle, punch through both layers of the belt at the same time. Repeat for the second hole.

Attaching the Buckle

We are using snaps here, but the process is very similar for rivets. Simply follow these steps and add a rivet everywhere we press a snap together.

1. With the finished sides of the buckle and belt facing upward, feed the buckle end of the belt around the bar on the buckle.

2. Push the buckle tongue through the oblong hole.

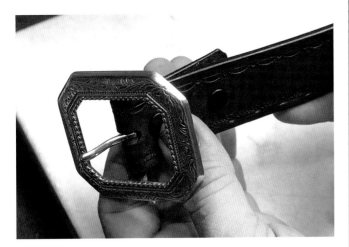

3. Press the snaps closest to the buckle together.

4. Thread the keeper up to the first snap.

5. Press the second snap together.

6. The belt is finished and ready to wear.

Making a Belt Keeper

Belt keepers sold by leathercraft vendors don't cost much, but they are typically stapled rather than sewn. Using a belt keeper block is optional, but it will come in handy if you plan to make many belts and keepers. This measured drawing will accommodate 1-inch to 1¹/₄-inch keepers. The dimensions can be adjusted for other size keepers.

1. Start with a leather strip ¹/₂ inch wide by about 6 inches. Use a 2 edge beveler to bevel the top and bottom edges of the strip.

2. Size the keeper by wrapping it tightly around a folded buckle end, as shown.

Belt Keeper Block

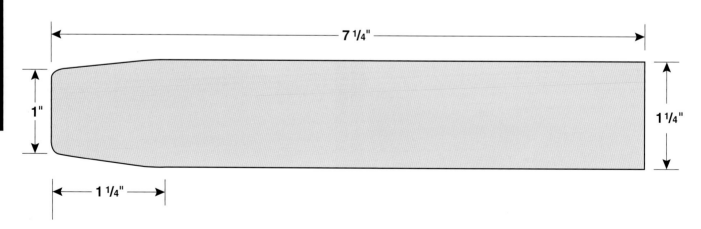

Make from ³/₈"-thick material (hardwood)

NOTE: This block is for a 1"–1¹/₄" keeper—adjust dimensions for other sizes
Use ³/₈" wood for all blockers

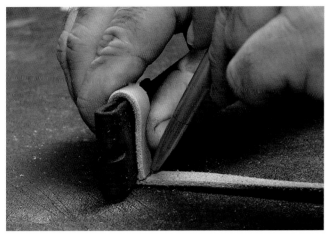

3. Use a ballpoint pen, awl, or other implement to make a mark where the leather meets.

4. Use scissors to cut at the mark.

Tools and Supplies

- ☐ ¹/₂- by 6-inch, 4-ounce cowhide strip
- ☐ Size 2 edge beveler
- ☐ Leather shears
- ☐ Skiver
- ☐ Punch awl
- ☐ Soap bar
- ☐ Leather Weld
- ☐ Stitching needle
- ☐ 10-inch length waxed linen thread
- ☐ Two segments of belt leather or belt keeper block

5. The two ends will be joined end-to-end as shown.

6. With the flesh side facing up, skive one end at about a 30-degree angle. This is most easily accomplished with the leather supported at the edge of the work surface, as shown.

7. Your belt keeper now has one skived end and one straight end.

8. With the grain side up, skive the opposite end at about a 30-degree angle.

9. The two ends will now join together perfectly.

10. Use a stylus, awl tip, or pen to make four marks $1/4$ inch from each end and slightly in from each edge to serve as stitching placement marks.

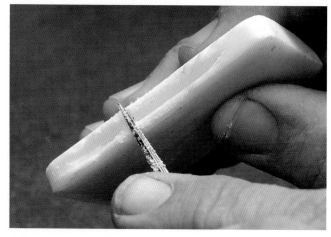

11. Apply ordinary bar soap to the end of a stitching awl.

152

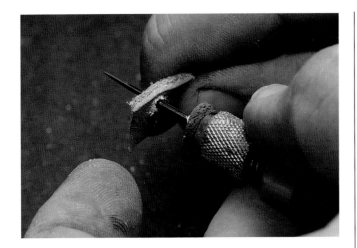

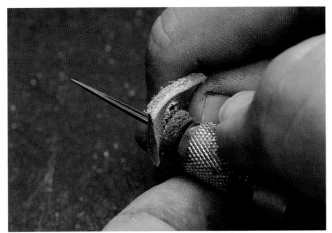

12. Hold the awl so that the top edge of the awl blade is parallel to the edge of the leather as shown and punch through the leather on all four marks.

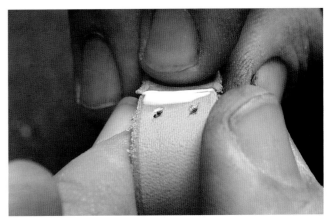

13. Apply Leather Weld or other similar leather glue to one skived end and press together. Hold the joint together until the glue sets well enough to hold the pieces together. For best results, allow to dry overnight before proceeding.

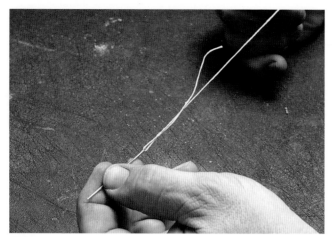

14. Thread the needle with a 10-inch length of waxed linen thread.

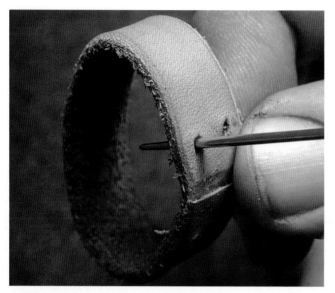

15. Insert the needle in the upper left hole and pull it through, leaving a 2-inch tail in the front.

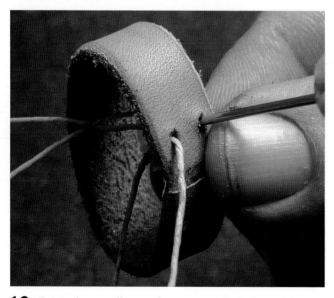

16. Bring the needle out the upper right hole and draw the thread tight.

17. Insert the needle in the lower left hole and draw the thread tight.

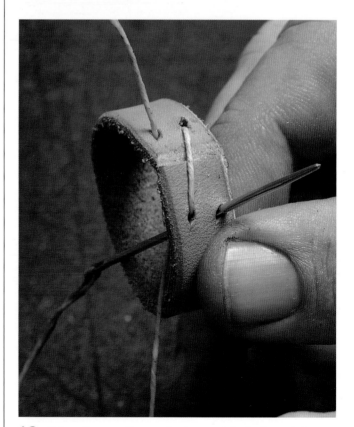

18. Bring the needle out the lower right hole and draw the thread tight.

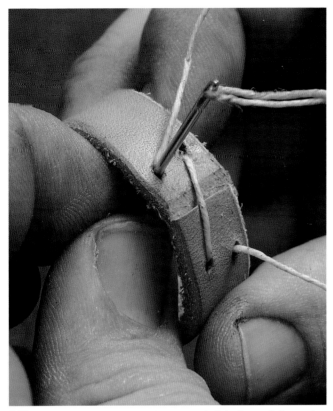

19. Insert the needle in the upper left hole and draw the thread tight.

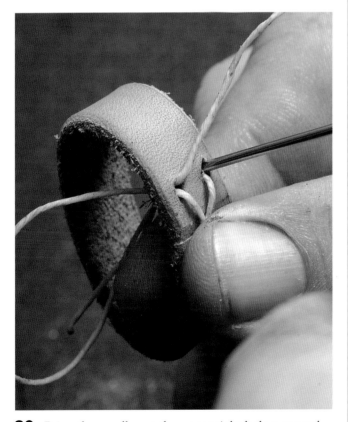

20. Bring the needle out the upper right hole a second time and draw the thread tight.

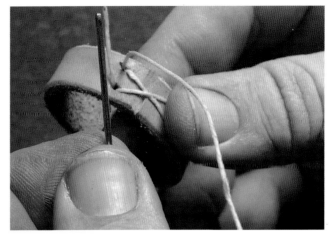

21. Remove the thread from the needle.

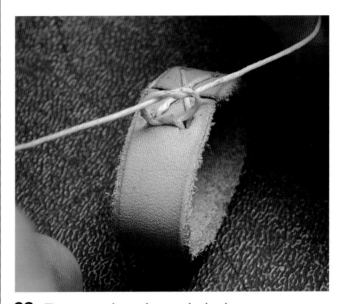

22. Tie a square knot close to the leather.

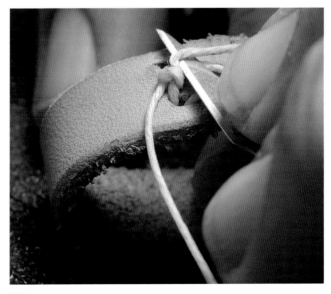

23. Cut the thread ends close to the knot.

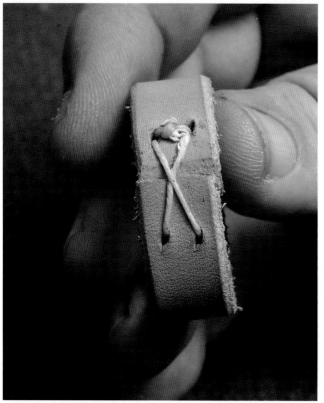

24. The finished keeper is ready to dye to match your belt. Let the keeper dry for 24 hours after dyeing.

26. Push the keeper onto a block until it fits snugly and let dry overnight. An alternative to using a block is to place the keeper on two pieces of leather that are the same thickness as your belt. The results won't be quite as good but will suffice.

25. Thoroughly wet the keeper in hot water.

Once you learn the basic carving and stamping techniques, you can create an infinite number of one-of-a-kind belt designs similar to these done by leathercrafter Bill Hollis. Here is just a small sampling of what can be done with a fresh belt blank and a few leathercraft tools.

A design is similar to the demo project, made with Craftools V-407, C-834, S-724, and P-703. The design was embellished with random peaks and valleys made by the pear shader.

Only two Craftools were used to make this basketweave design: D-436 and X-534. The edge stitching dresses up the belt.

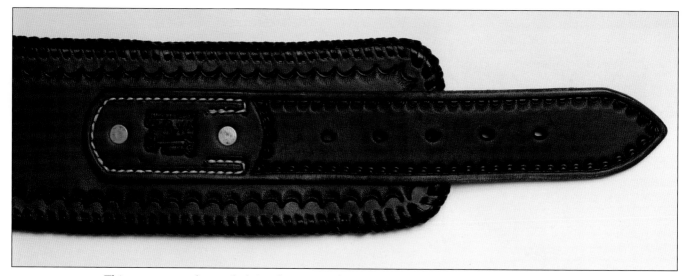

This western-style gun belt is a bit more advanced, but the stamping is straightforward. Experiment with your favorite camouflage and border tools to produce your own unique design. The stamping on this belt was made with Craftools D-438 and D-435.

These belts feature western floral-style carving. To get good at this type of design, you need to practice, practice, practice. The flowers, leaves, and stems are beveled, providing dimension by raising them off the leather surface. Pear shaders give the leaves and petals curvature and more depth. The veiner tool makes leaves appear curved, while the camouflage tool adds interest. The seeders add realism to the flower centers. And finally, the background stamping draws attention to the main figures.

Tools and Supplies

- ☐ Smooth marble, polyester, or other hard surface for stamping.
- ☐ 4-ounce cowhide leather rectangle 4$\frac{1}{4}$ inches wide by 5$\frac{1}{4}$ inches long
- ☐ Moroccan or other lining leather 5 inches long by 6$\frac{1}{2}$ inches wide
- ☐ Card case pattern (from page 162)
- ☐ 4-ounce scrap leather for testing stamps
- ☐ Skiver
- ☐ Size 2 edge beveler
- ☐ Leather shears
- ☐ Utility knife or head knife
- ☐ Swivel knife

- ☐ Beveler tools and a border tool or stamps of your choice (Craftool B203, B701, and D436 were used here).
- ☐ Modeling tool with medium ball end
- ☐ Three-dimensional stamp of your choice (the Marine Corps logo was used here)
- ☐ Stitching groover
- ☐ 4-in-1 stitching awl set or stitching awl with a size 2 blade
- ☐ Stitching wheel
- ☐ Scratch awl or stylus
- ☐ Wing dividers
- ☐ Single-edge razor blade
- ☐ Leather conditioner (such as Lexol)

- ☐ Gel Antique (saddle tan was used here)
- ☐ Small jar or tube of acrylic paint (metallic gold was used here)
- ☐ 60-grit sandpaper
- ☐ Edge wax and burnishing cloth
- ☐ Edge Kote
- ☐ Bone tool
- ☐ Small bowl of clean water and cellulose sponge
- ☐ Measuring square
- ☐ Cotton swabs
- ☐ Ballpoint pen
- ☐ Stitching needles
- ☐ Waxed nylon thread

Putting It All Together

Card Case Pattern

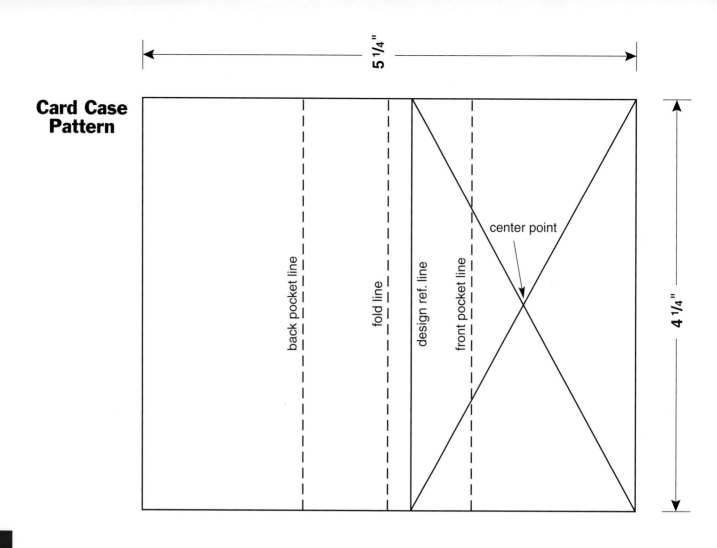

5 1/4"

4 1/4"

back pocket line

fold line

design ref. line

front pocket line

center point

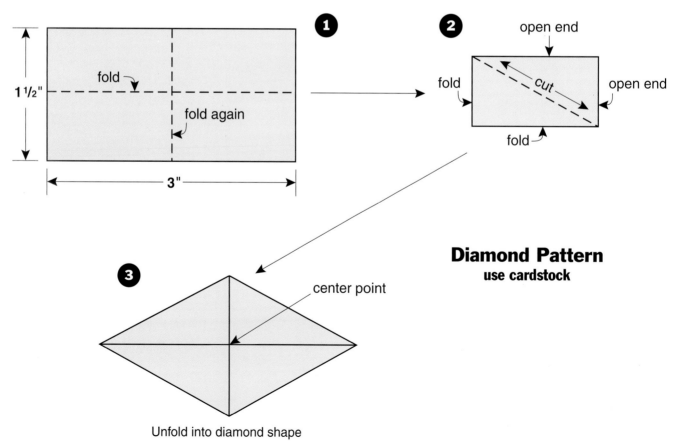

❶

1 1/2"

fold

fold again

3"

❷

open end

fold

cut

open end

fold

❸

center point

Diamond Pattern
use cardstock

Unfold into diamond shape

1. Prepare the leather for stamping as instructed previously. Wet the leather with clean water and sponge. When the entire piece is evenly wet, spray on a generous amount of leather conditioner. Gently rub in the leather conditioner in a circular motion, using your fingers, until it is all absorbed.

2. Use a stitching groover and stitching wheel to prepare the piece to be stitched.

3. Place the card case pattern over the leather, matching up the edges.

4. Use the awl to lightly mark the center point of the card case front by punching through the pattern onto the leather.

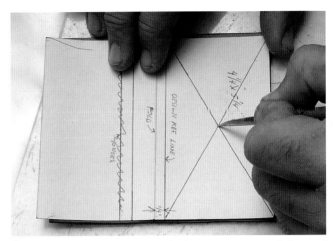

5. Find the center of the diamond pattern piece

6. Use the awl or stylus to hold down the pattern at the center mark. Arrange the diamond so it is centered properly within the three grooves. Use a divider arm or stylus to mark one of the diamond points. Without moving the pattern, use the awl or stylus to mark the other three points of the diamond.

7. While holding the pattern down firmly so it doesn't move, use your awl or stylus to very lightly trace the pattern. Don't cut into the leather or press too deeply.

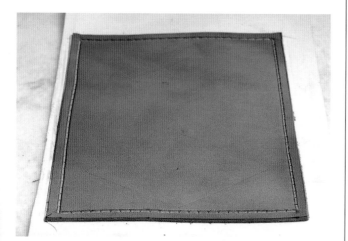

8. This is how your project should look at this stage.

1. Strop the swivel knife. This will help your knife blade cut smoothly through the leather.

2. Starting in one corner, follow your guideline and cut a clear, clean line. Each side of the diamond should be made in one smooth cut.

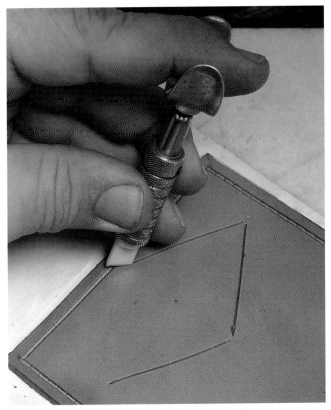

3. Stop at the next corner and lift your knife up.

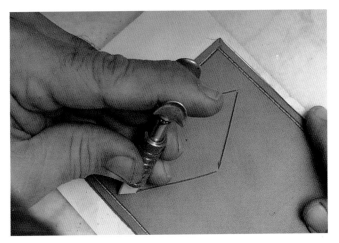

4. Replace the corner edge of the knife at this corner mark but make sure to leave a space so that the lines do not touch.

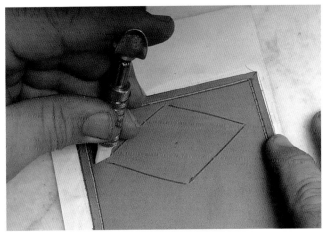

5. Repeat the process on the other sides of the triangle.

6. Prepare your Craftool beveler tool B 201. Strop the bottom and side edges of the tool. Note that the beveler tool is the only stamping tool you will strop.

7. Wipe off excess jeweler's rogue.

8. Place your beveler at a 90-degree angle with the edge placed along the inside of your triangle. Start at a corner and move the beveler smoothly along the line as you make short, light taps. Stop when you reach the end of the cut.

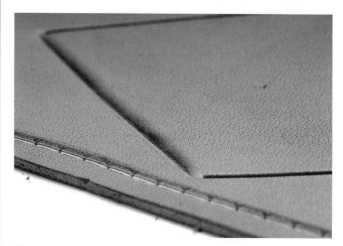

9. This is how your beveled line should look.

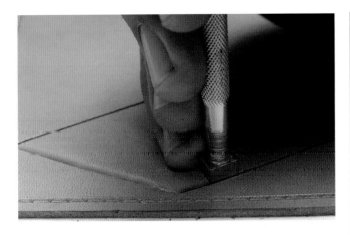

10. Place your tool at the beginning of the second side of the triangle and bevel to the end. Be sure to stop at the end of the cut, leaving a small space between the diamond sides.

11. The beveled edges should appear straight and of equal depth.

12. Continue beveling the remaining two sides of the diamond.

13. To add interest, switch to the texture beveling tool, Craftool B701. Re-bevel all edges using the same technique you used with the smooth beveler.

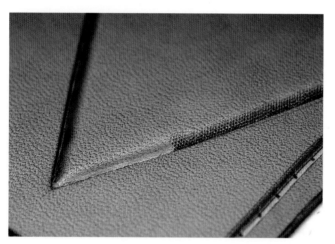

14. Notice the difference between a straight beveled edge on the left portion of the cut and after using a texture beveler, shown on the right portion of the cut.

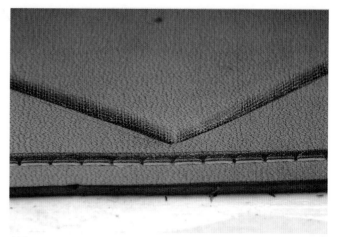

15. By leaving a space between the cuts, you should get a nice crisp corner on your diamond.

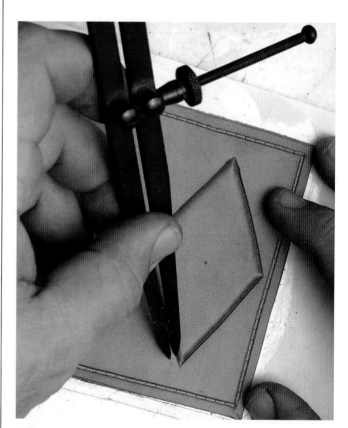

16. To add interest to the design, create a second diamond on the outside of the first diamond. This also shows that you don't always have to bevel against a cut line.

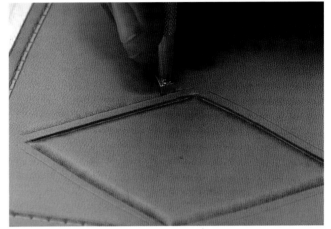

17. Set the divider arms about ³/₁₆ inch apart. Place one arm in the cut and pull toward you, letting the weight of the other arm make a slight impression in the leather. Repeat this process on all sides.

18. Use the Craftool texture beveler B701 to gently bevel against the line. Go slowly, carefully obliterating the line as you go. When you reach a corner, lift the tool and set it down at the correct angle on the line. Because there is not a cut line, it is not necessary to leave a gap between where one line ends and the other begins.

19. Allow the bevel to taper off as you reach the stitching guideline.

20. Use the modeling tool with the medium ball end to enhance and smooth the inside cut line, which has already been beveled.

21. Select the three-dimensional stamp of your choice. Center the stamp by eye within the triangle. If the numbers and writing are right side up with the project facing you, the stamp is in the proper orientation. Without moving the stamp, insert the handle. If the stamp moves, readjust it.

22. With the handle at a 90-degree angle, hold down tight and hit the handle hard with the mallet three times.

23. Without lifting or moving the stamp, hit the stamp hard a couple of times at each clock position in this order: 12 o'clock, 6 o'clock, 9 o'clock, and 3 o'clock.

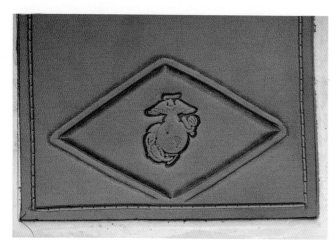

24. Remove the stamp and check the results. If any portion of the stamp is too light, carefully register the stamp and rap again with the mallet. The stamp must be positioned exactly or you will make a double impression, which will be difficult, if not impossible, to fix.

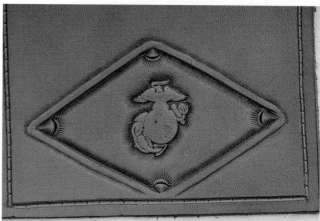

26. The border tool D436 will add more interest to the design. Stamp the design in all four corners.

25. Use the texture beveler Craftool B 701 to bevel around the edge of the 3-D stamp. Move the tool along carefully, using the corner of the tool to get into any tight areas of the design.

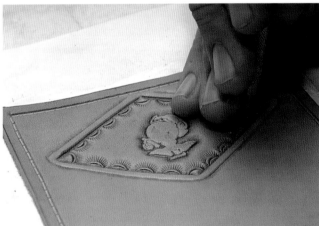

27. Continue stamping the design along the cut line, using your eye to judge the spacing. With this tool, four impressions may be made between the corner stamps. When you are experimenting with your own tools and designs, the way to achieve success is by preparing a sample test piece and through practice.

Coloring the Case

1. Let your project dry for several hours or overnight before dying. Apply gel antique evenly over the entire card case. Be sure to work the gel into the recessed areas of the stamp. Inspect the stamped areas and if any spots were missed, apply more gel where needed, rub in, and rub off.

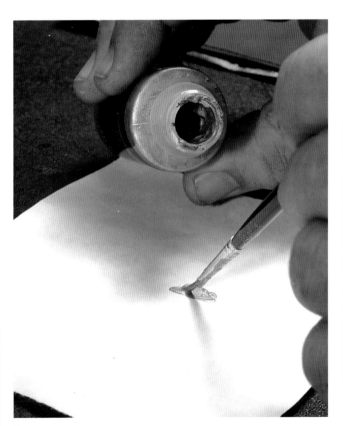

2. A metallic gold accent color will be added to the stamped emblem after the antique gel is dry. Place a small amount of metallic gold acrylic paint on a card or paper plate. If it's too thick, add a drop or two of water.

3. A small liner brush is used to paint the stamped area. If you accidentally paint outside of the stamped area, wipe the paint off right away with a slightly damp cloth or paper towel.

4. Acrylic paint dries quickly. When it is dry to the touch, remove the cardstock backing by pulling up on one of the short ends until you can grasp the case. Pull the cardstock off slowly while holding the case in your other hand.

Preparing and Attaching the Lining

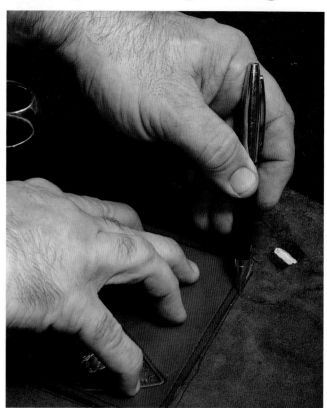

1. Black Moroccan leather is used to line this project. Use a ballpoint pen to trace the outline of the card case on the flesh side of the lining leather.

2. Cut about 1 inch away from the lines on all sides.

3. Use pushpins to pin the lining, flesh side up, to your rubber mat. Use as many pins as needed to hold the lining taut—there must be no wrinkles.

4. Use a wool dauber to apply two coats of solvent-based cement on the flesh sides of the liner and card case. Follow the directions on the product's packaging for this procedure. Be sure to cover the entire lining and card case with the cement.

5. Let the pieces dry to the touch after the second coat of cement has been applied.

6. You can tell if the cement is ready by touching the surface. It should be tacky but none should come off on your finger.

7. Once you place the tooled leather piece on the lining, it cannot be adjusted. Start by placing just the edge of the tooled leather piece onto the liner. Getting it to lie precisely on the line is not essential.

8. Begin pressing the piece down with your finger from one end to the other while holding the loose end away from the cemented portion of the liner.

9. Push down edges all the way around the case using your finger.

10. Remove the pushpins and check your lining. Because the cement extended past the edge of your tooled leather piece, the liner should be firmly adhered to the edges. To remove the excess liner, use a sharp razor blade.

11. Punch the tip of the blade up through the liner along the edge of the stamped piece. Begin slicing it off by pulling the blade toward you, keeping the blade against the heavier leather. Continue in this manner until the liner is removed from all four sides.

12. If your blade is sharp, the edges of the liner and the heavy leather should be exactly even.

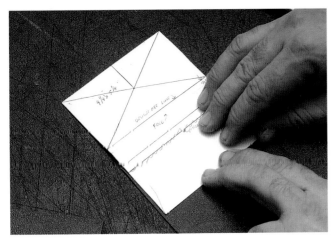

13. Now you will make the pockets from the same leather as the lining. To make them easier to attach, you will want to cut the pockets ¼ to ½ inch larger than the pattern on the two sides.

Start with a piece of lining leather about 5 inches wide that aready has one straight edge.

14. Place your pattern on the leather, lining up the straight edge with the top of the pocket. Place your ruler right against the edge of the pattern.

15. Remove the pattern without moving the ruler and cut out the rectangle using a razor blade or rotary cutter. Repeat the process for the second pocket.

16. You should now have two pockets that are the same size.

17. Stack the pockets on top of one another with the edges even.

CUTTING THUMB HOLES

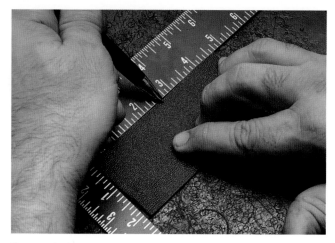

1. Mark the center of one of the long edges on the flesh side with a pen.

2. To make the arc of the thumbhole, center a quarter over the mark.

3. Trace the outline onto the leather.

4. Cut out carefully along the line using leather shears.

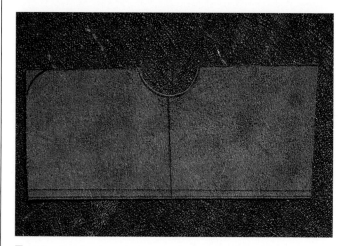

5. The finished card case pockets with thumbhole.

Cutting Thumb Holes with a Punch

An alternate method is to use a half round strap end punch. You may not want to buy one just for this purpose, but if you have one on hand, it is a quick, professional way to cut thumb holes.

Mark the center of a long edge of one of the pocket pieces on the flesh side. Place both pocket pieces together, matching the top, bottom, and sides. Center the punch over the center mark and tap with the mallet, using moderate pressure. Both thumbholes are complete.

Gluing

1. To prepare the piece for gluing, first identify the space on the card case between the two pockets. To do this, place them on the lined side of the card case, with the bottom edges even.

2. Use a pen to make a mark on the card case liner to show where the top edge will be on each side. Repeat this step for the second pocket.

3. Use coarse 60- to 80-grit sandpaper to roughen up about ⅛ inch along the edge of the card case liner.

4. Do not sand between the marks you made that designated where the pockets end, as it will show once the pockets are added.

5. The next step is to glue the pockets to the card case using white leather glue. Spread a small puddle of glue onto freezer paper, paper plate, or other disposable item. With a craft stick or something similar, spread a line of glue along the sanded portions of the edges.

6. Stop the glue line at your marks.

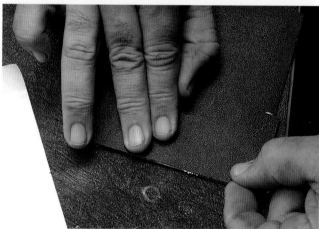

7. Position the pocket so that the thumbhole is in the center of the case, leaving the extra leather sticking out on the outer edges. Make sure the top edge of the pocket lines up with the pocket liner indication marks on the lining. Press down firmly.

8. Some of the glue should squeeze out around the edges.

9. Use a toothpick to wipe off the excess glue.

10. Complete the second pocket in the same way. Make sure all the glue has been cleaned off the edges, then let dry overnight.

Finishing the Case

1. Now that the lining is cemented and the pockets are secured with glue, the project is ready to be stitched. Stitch all four sides of the card case.

2. Trim off the excess pocket material. Place the case with the tooled side up on your cutting board. Hold the case down firmly with one hand. Place a utility knife along the edge of the tooled leather piece and cut off the entire pocket excess.

3. To set the fold, wet the entire tooled side of the card case under running water.

4. Even up the edges of the case.

5. Firmly press the folded edge with your fingers to set the fold. Towel off excess water if necessary. Place waxed paper over the case and weigh it down with any flat, heavy object, such as the stone slab, and let it dry overnight. Apply a finishing product such as Leather Balm with Atom Wax.

Once you've learned the basics of leathercrafting, you don't have to stop with the belt and card case projects demonstrated here. Combine all of the techniques to make many other leather accessories. Here are just a few to provide you with some inspiration.

Checkbook Cover

Key Case

Three-ring Binder Cover and Wallet

Center-bar Belt Buckles

Holster

Kinfe Sheath

Clutch purse

Resources

This list is a starting point for locating leather suppliers and experts. With a little research, you will find other online vendors and perhaps a shop near your home. If you enjoy working and socializing with others, check out the leatherworking guild Internet sites. There you will find more resources and regional leathercraft groups who conduct regular information–sharing meetings and sponsor other events and activities. If there are no groups in your area, consider starting your own club. You may be surprised at how many people are engaged in this centuries-old craft and wish to share their knowledge and accomplishments.

Barry King Tools
Quality stainless-steel stamping tools
www.barrykingtools.com
Email: kingtool@fiberpipe.net
Store: 1751 Terra Avenue
Sheridan, WY 82801
Phone: 307-672-5657

Big House Daddy Leather
Project patterns
www.bighousedaddy.com
Phone: 614-468-1323

Brettuns Village Leather
Complete line of hides, tools, and supplies
www.brettunsvillage.com/leather
Email: leather@brettunsvillage.com
Store: 557 Lincoln Street
Lewiston, ME 04240
Phone: 207-782-7863

Craft Fair
Links to leathercraft suppliers in the United Kingdom
www.craft-fair.co.uk/

eLeather Supply
Complete line of hides, tool, supplies, and more
www.eleathersupply.com
Email: info@eleathersupply.com
Phone: 512-686-3699

HideCrafter Leather Company
Hides, tools, patterns, and more
Internet: www.hidecrafter.com
Email: eric@hidecrafter.com
Store: 7936 Camp Bowie West Blvd.
Fort Worth, TX 76116
Phone: 817-878-5797

Just Leather.com
Hides, lining leathers, and more
www.justleather.com
E-mail: info@justleather.com
Phone & fax 207-641-8313

Leather Cord USA
Lacing and cording
www.leathercordusa.com
Email: sales@leathercordusa.com
Store: 503 Hickory Ridge Trail, Suite 110
Woodstock, GA 30188
Phone: 770-928-3993
Toll Free: 877-700-2673

Leather Unlimited
Hides, tools, and supplies
www.leatherunltd.com
service@leatherunltd.com
Phone: 920-994-9464

Montana Leather
Complete line of hides, tools, and supplies
Phone: 406 245-1660
Toll free: 800-527-0227
Internet: www.montanaleather.com
E-Mail mail@montanaleather.com
Store: 2015 1st Ave. N
Billings, MT 59103

S&D Trading Company
Complete line of hides, tools, and supplies
www.sdtradingco.com
Phone: 806-795-6062

Springfield Leather Company
Complete line of hides, tools, and supplies; membership
    club offering discounted merchandise
www.springfieldleather.com
Phone: 417-881-0223
Toll Free: 800-668-8518
Store: 1463 S. Glenstone
Springfield, MO 65808

Standing Bear's Trading Post
Complete line of hides, tools, supplies, and more;
    free patterns
www.sbearstradingpost.com
Email: inquiry@sbearstradingpost.com
Phone: 818 342-9120
Store: 7624 Tampa Ave.
Reseda, CA 91335

Tandy Leather Factory
Complete line of hides, lining leathers, tools, patterns,
    supplies, and more
www.tandyleatherfactory.com
Stores: More than 100 locations in the U.S., Canada, and
    the United Kingdom

Trigg Leather
Primarily lining, garment, and upholstery leather; also
    buckles and a good selection of conchos
http://triggleather.net/index2.php
Email: info@triggleather.net
Store: 1213 N. Chadbourne St.
San Angelo, TX 76903
Phone: 325-653-1212
Toll free phone: 877-95-TRIGG (USA Only)

Wylie Leather Works
Belt blanks, buckles, tools, kits
www.wylieleatherworks.com
Email: info@wylieleatherworks.com
Phone: 505-281-5822

Leathercraft Groups

The International Federation of Leather Guilds
www.ifolg.org

International Internet Leathercrafters Guild
http://iilg.org/
Email: president@iilg.net

The Leathercraft Guild
www.theleathercraftguild.com
Email: leatherguild@verizon.net

Museum of Leathercraft
Virtual gallery of leather artifacts
www.museumofleathercraft.org/
Abington Museum, Abington Park, Northampton. U.K.